Tim,
Ride well!

7/28/10

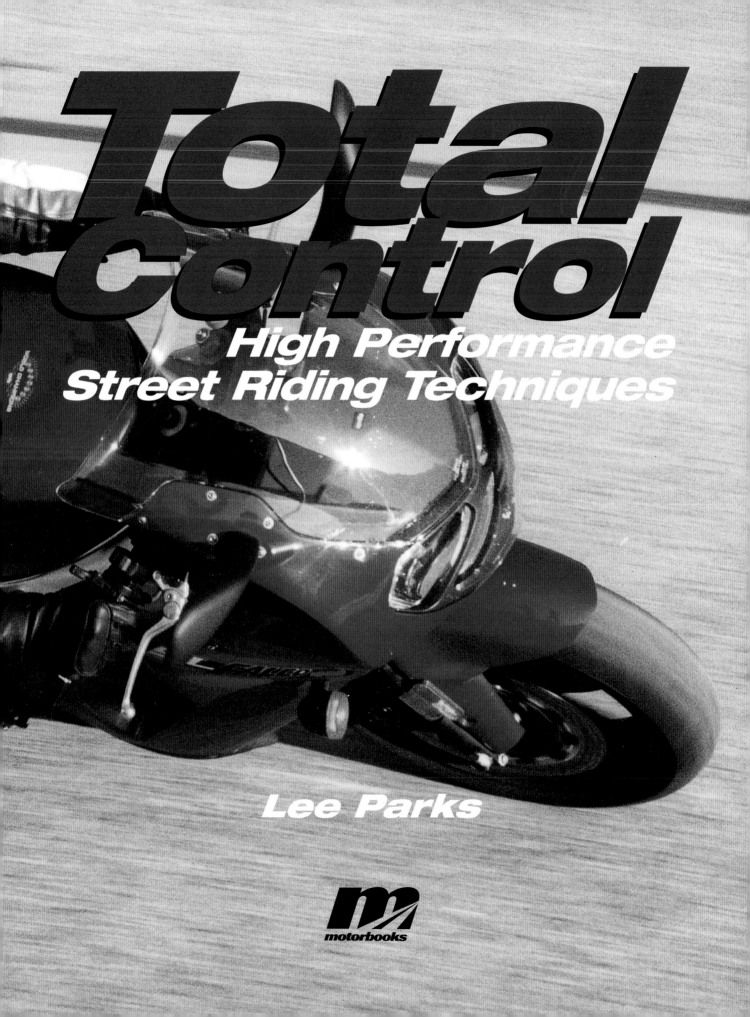

Total Control

High Performance Street Riding Techniques

Lee Parks

motorbooks

This edition first published in 2003 by MBI Publishing Company
and Motorbooks, an imprint of MBI Publishing Company, 400 1st
Avenue North, Suite 300, Minneapolis, MN 55401 USA

The information in this book is true and complete to the best of our
knowledge. All recommendations are made without any guarantee
on the part of the author or Publisher, who also disclaim any liability
incurred in connection with the use of this data or specific details.

We recognize that some words, model names and designations,
for example, mentioned herein are the property of the trademark
holder. We use them for identification purposes only. This is not
an official publication.

Motorbooks titles are also available at discounts in bulk quantity
for industrial or sales-promotional use. For details write to Special
Sales Manager at MBI Publishing Company, 400 1st Avenue
North, Suite 300, Minneapolis, MN 55401 USA.

To find out more about our books, join us online at
www.motorbooks.com.

Edited by Darwin Holmstrom and Kent Larson
Designed by Tom Heffron
Layout by Katie Sonmor and Brenda Canales

ISBN-13: 978-0-7603-1403-6

Printed in Hong Kong

Contents

Foreword

By Darwin Holmstrom

Although it's taken me the better part of forty years, I've finally discovered one great truth about riding a motorcycle: I still have a hell of a lot to learn. I've been riding since the age of 11, and I've lived and breathed motorcycles even longer than that (I've actually authored a book called *The Complete Idiot's Guide to Motorcycles*), so this was quite a realization.

This shift in my universe came about as a result of my finally being exposed to road racing. I'd always been a standard or sport-touring kind of rider, one of those guys who relished 1,000-mile days. My dreams of glory involved winning the Iron Butt Rally, not winning any road racing championships. Up until a few years ago the most sporting motorcycle I'd ever owned had been a Honda ST1100. Then, a few years ago, I discovered Speedvision (now Speed Channel). Suddenly motorcycle road racing was no longer some remote activity that I read about in the back pages of *Cycle World*, months after the fact. Now a coaxial cable was bringing same-day coverage of that racing right into my living room.

Speedvision was the first step down a slippery slope. I began hanging with a bad crowd. I'm not talking about the flip-flop-wearing squids riding 100-mile-per-hour wheelies on metropolitan freeways. I fell in with some serious Sportbike riders, mature, highly skilled folks, many of whom had at least an amateur road-racing license. With very few exceptions, these are sensible men and women who practice sound riding techniques. They just practice them at a very high level. To become a responsible member of this group meant I had to take my own skills to a higher level.

My experience is not uncommon. Every year it seems as though more and more people are motivated to ride at a higher level. Unfortunately, far too often this motivation manifests itself in the purchase of the latest and greatest technology. Many riders think the key to riding better is to purchase better equipment. They purchase this week's fastest open-class Sportbike or the hottest new 600cc machine. They spend small fortunes upgrading their motorcycles with top-shelf suspension components sold by companies that spell their names with umlauts. They increase the power output of machines that are already too fast for their level of riding ability. Undoubtedly, better equipment makes it easier to ride at a higher level, but only if the rider possesses the skill to ride at that level. Simply throwing money at a lack of skill won't help a bit.

Perhaps because I lacked the small fortune necessary to pursue the latest and greatest technology, I chose to take my riding to a higher level by concentrating on improving my skills. I swallowed my pride and began to ask questions of the best riders in our group, not worrying about whether or not those questions were stupid. More importantly, I listened to their answers with an open mind, and went out and practiced the techniques they advised.

I began investigating high-performance riding classes. To my great surprise, one of the most highly recommended riding classes was the Advanced Riding Clinic taught by none other than my old friend Lee Parks.

By this time I had taken a job as an acquisitions editor at Motorbooks International. My job involved conceiving book ideas and finding people to write them. The next step didn't require an extraordinary amount of thought. Lee teaches a highly respected high-performance riding course. Lee is a talented and experienced writer. Obviously, Lee should write this book. Which he did. Although Lee's busy schedule and his meticulous attention to detail meant that the book took some time to create (and gave me an ulcer big enough to run an Aprilia Mille exhaust header through), the result exceeded my wildest expectations.

You hold in your hands the result of a lifetime of thought and experience. You hold the key to becoming a better, faster, and safer rider. When I first began watching people like Colin Edwards and Nicky Hayden race, it seemed that the things they did on a motorcycle were completely impossible. This book demystifies the skills practiced by such riders. While this book won't turn you into Valentino Rossi overnight, you will learn the same basic skills Rossi uses when practicing his craft. In *Total Control*, Parks breaks down the elements of high-performance riding into easily understood steps that anyone can master if willing to practice them. I have been amazed at how practicing these exercises has improved my own riding skills. Even though I still don't have the best and brightest Sportbike on the market—I ride a Yamaha YZF600R—I now find I'm waiting at stop signs for riders who used to leave me behind. I hope you find this volume as useful and practical as I have. Ride safe.

Acknowledgments

I originally figured that writing this book would be a cakewalk given that it was simply supposed to be a written version of my Advanced Riding Clinics (ARC), which I know like the back of my hand. I could not have been more wrong. Fortunately, I am blessed with amazing friends and family whose outstanding support helped make this book a reality.

First and foremost, I'd like to thank my editor, Darwin Holmstrom. Not only did he convince me to do this book in the first place, but he proceeded to kick me in the butt on a weekly and even daily basis for close to a year until I finally got it finished. Without his efforts, this book would still be a wistful fantasy.

Next I'd like to thank Race Tech founder Paul Thede who showed his selfless nature by allowing me to take a career's worth of his writing and whittle it down into the two suspension chapters, which are better than I ever could have done on my own.

Also high on the list are those friends who contributed their time, expertise, principles, and words to help make sure the book was both accurate and completed on time. My engineering editor, Ray Engelhardt, took on the daunting task of explaining many physics principles to me without the aid of mathematics. It's amazing either of us survived it. My fellow ARC instructors Tracy Martin and Ed Pearsell not only helped me shape and teach the curriculum, but also acted as photo models for many of the shots. NESBA control rider Kent Larson contributed chapter 21, Track Days. Tom Riles taught me all I know about action photography. Terry McGarry, L.T. Snyder, D.C. Wilson, Ken Marena, Jason Elzaurdia, Peter Tavernise, Priscilla Wong, Debbie Webber, Amy Holland, Kevin Cameron, Kevin Wing, Andy Goldfine, Mansoor Shafi, Denise Sullivan, Randy Hatch, Kent Soignier, Michael Martinucci, and Kim Andersen also made contributions too numerous to detail. And a special thanks goes to the folks at Avon tires for contributing many photos to the cause.

Of course, I have to thank my parents for allowing me the privilege of riding motorcycles at a young age. My dad taught me the basics of riding and supported my two-wheeled addiction until I could afford to do it on my own. He also gave me my first professional writing, editing, and graphic design jobs and taught me how to use a camera. My mom spent many weekends transporting my friends and me to the local motocross track and tried to read her novels as we made lots of noise and covered her in dust. She also taught me most of what I know about teaching.

I can't stress enough the contribution of my students over the years. Through them I was able to refine the riding and teaching techniques until they just plain worked. I easily learned as much from them as they did from me.

Although much of the riding technology in this book is original thought, it has been built on the extensive bodies of research of those who have come before me. In a letter to colleague Robert Hook on February 5, 1676, Sir Isaac Newton said "If I have seen further it is by standing on the shoulders of giants." In that spirit, I would like to acknowledge my giants: Keith Code, David Hough, and Freddie Spencer. On many occasions here they are quoted or credited with words or ideas, but anyone familiar with their work will recognize their collective influence throughout this book. It would not have happened without their individual contributions to my riding and thinking.

Finally, I'd like to acknowledge Landmark Education (www.landmarkeducation.com) and its Curriculum for Living. This work made my career possible.

I'm sure my mediocre memory has left out some other important people who in one way or another contributed to the creation of this book. So I apologize, in advance, for their omission. Obviously, a lifetime of experiences and interactions with my fellow earthlings can't be summed up in a single page of text. If nothing else, this book is a testament to the generosity of the human spirit. Thanks to you all.

Introduction

The speed and capabilities of modern motorcycles now far exceed the average rider's abilities. In fact, the difference between stock street bikes and full-blown racing superbikes is a tiny fraction of that between sports cars and their racing counterparts. This has created a need for more and better rider education.

The Problem of Learning to Go Fast

Having spent many years in riding and racing schools, I am a big supporter of rider training. The knowledge I have gleaned from these classes has literally saved my life numerous times. For a sport rider who wants to improve his technique (especially high-speed cornering), there are two basic options: the Motorcycle Safety Foundation Experienced RiderCourse and the various track schools. Unfortunately, while both are worthwhile, each has drawbacks that limit how much a rider can improve by participating.

The problem with the MSF ERC (although I highly recommend it) is that all the drills are at such low speeds that the fear of going fast is never handled, and the advanced skills used by racers to control their bikes at high speeds are not taught. Track schools, on the other hand, have the opposite problem. The speeds are so much higher than most street riders are used to that many are afraid to try new techniques for fear of a high-speed crash. This is a real shame as most track schools have solid skills to teach, but the racetrack environment is not ideal for the average street rider to learn the basics of high-performance riding. Once a rider has the basics down, however, there is nothing better than a good track school to refine and expand on those skills.

As part of my duties as Editor of *Motorcycle Consumer News* from 1995–2000, I had the privilege of working with both David Hough and Keith Code on many riding skill articles. They really sparked my interest in the subject. Even though I finished 2nd overall in the AMA 125 GP nationals in 1994, I realized while working on these articles that although I was fast, I still had much to learn about how to control a motorcycle. I became concerned because I mostly learned how to race by "feel" and wasn't entirely sure exactly what I was doing. This made my riding inconsistent. When I had problems on a particular track, I didn't know how to diagnose

them, let alone fix them. Long conversations with Hough and Code finally got me thinking about the physical dynamics of riding and I began a quest to figure out an easy way to fix my riding when necessary.

A New Way to Learn

As it turns out, many of our readers were also looking for a similar "easy" way to improve their riding. I kept getting complaints from street riders that there was too big a gap between the MSF ERC and the track schools. Some wished for a "middle step," and others had no interest in ever going on a track—despite my encouragement—and just wanted something a little "stronger" than the ERC. To make things worse, many also complained that the only books on the subject were written for racers and were too complicated for them. They wanted simpler solutions for high-performance street riding, not sophisticated racing strategies.

After listening to enough of these "middle-stepper" complaints, I eventually decided to do something about it and began work on a new genre of riding school. It would combine the advanced techniques of the track schools, with the lower-stress parking lot environment of the ERC. Just as importantly, each skill would be broken down to its simplest form and practiced individually in a building block format.

Using many friends as guinea pigs, the curriculum and drills began to take shape. My basic teaching philosophy was simple. Rather than ask a rider to try something at, say, 20 mph faster than he ever has tried such an exercise before (which happens at some track schools), I would ask the student to try going faster in small, 2-mph increments. This prevented him from getting too scared.

For example, let's say that a full race pace around a 40-foot diameter circle is around 32 mph. A typical street rider might be comfortable going around it at 17 mph. The important thing here is to keep the student comfortable so he will be willing to try something new. First, I teach the proper technique at 0 mph. To do this I have the student get on his bike and along with several other students to help me, we go through a mock turn by leaning the bike all the way over and back up while I help properly position the rider's body in real time. We do this several times until the student can do

The author has raced motorcycles since the age of 14. He won a national endurance championship in 2001.

everything right in the mock turn. Then he goes on the range and does it. After going 17 mph, he moves to 19, then to 21. Let's say he has a problem at 21 mph, I work with him on the problem until he can go 21 mph without a hitch. Then we move to 23, etc. Now he will likely not get to 32, but by the end of the day, using this teaching technique, each area of his riding will have made specific measurable improvements. My Advanced Riding Clinic (ARC) was born.

Hundreds of students later, this method has more than proven its mettle. In fact, while the curriculum was originally designed for street riders, many racers have found it equally effective at improving their riding skills.

I originally stumbled across this method while figuring out how to teach myself to drag my knee back in college. Next to my dorm was a big empty parking lot that was mostly used during sporting events. One day when there were no such events planned, I had the parking lot all to myself. I set up a practice turn with the use of a couple of strategically placed dirty sweatshirts. The important thing here is that I did not set up a "course" with multiple turn and braking points. I felt it best to keep it simple. With my turn in place, I took a few deep breaths, strapped on my helmet, leathers, boots, and gloves, and set off to explore uncharted lean angles.

After about five minutes of warming my tires by weaving back and forth like I'd seen racers do on TV, I began slowly increasing my speed. I found that I had to keep changing my body position to deal with the increased velocities, and just kept playing around until it felt comfortable for me. Of course, I had no idea what I was doing, and had no knowledgeable instructors to help guide me, but after about 30 minutes of this, I finally touched my knee to the ground and felt like I had achieved a great milestone in my life.

Rather than risk ruining the moment, I picked up my clothing, parked the bike and walked back to my dorm room, a new man. Every rider who has ever dragged his knee remembers his first time like it was yesterday. Part of the reason for this is that it often requires years of practice to work up to it. However, in one half-hour on a sunny Saturday afternoon, I was able to break the threshold, within a low-stress environment, and so can you. Fortunately for you, everything I was missing that day is clearly spelled out for you in this book.

The Book Is Born

After teaching many ARCs at rallies around the country, two things were clear: My students were making incredible

Author Lee Parks recieves his trophy for finishing 2nd in the 1994 AMA 125GP nationals.

improvements in their riding, and I could never teach enough classes to make much of an impact in the general motorcycling population. It was for the second reason that I never sought any publicity for my Clinics. I knew I didn't have time to fulfill the demand even if I wanted to.

The Internet threw a monkey wrench into the mix, however, as happy graduates were posting their incredible stories of improvement on Web sites all over the place. One of the people who happened to notice many of these postings was Motorbooks International Acquisitions Editor Darwin Holmstrom, who asked about the possibility of doing a book on the subject. Although I had considered doing a book at some point, his call brought the project to the front burner. After much thought, I realized that doing a book was the only way to get this riding technology to the masses, and so I began putting words to paper.

After finishing the initial research, I decided to thoroughly test each and every technique by returning to national road racing after a seven-year absence. I chose to compete in the WERA National Endurance Series because the large amounts of track time would give me the most opportunities to validate my findings. I joined the Speed Werks/Cyberlogtech team racing a Suzuki SV650 in the Lightweight class. My two teammates had just earned their expert licenses after just one season of racing as novices. Although I didn't think we would be contenders for the crown, I figured it was an ideal opportunity to test the techniques with several riders.

Amazingly enough, even with a rookie crew with no endurance racing experience, we managed to win the championship in our first effort as a team. Obviously, the technology was ready for publication. On a very somber note, our team owner Scott Gowland was killed two weeks before we won the championship he worked so hard to achieve. It is to his memory that this book is dedicated.

What It Is

The purpose of this book is to teach you how to have total control of your bike. So, what does total control mean? The best definition I've heard was told to me by California Superbike School Chief Instructor Cobie Fair: "Putting the bike where you want, when you want it." How you use that control will vary from rider to rider. You can use it to go faster with the same level of safety you currently have, or ride safer at the same speed, or some of both. This book deals specifically with riding technique, not racing strategy. That subject will be covered in another book.

This book gives you a real tool for making improvements in your riding. In doing so, it empowers you to self-diagnose problems when they occur, as well as giving you the solutions. In other words, you will learn specific riding techniques that will put you in control of your motorcycle. This is fundamentally different from giving you generic advice like "be smooth." I think Keith Code said it best when he called smoothness the "false promise" because, in and of itself, it doesn't tell you how to achieve this state. By practicing the specific techniques over and over, you will eventually perform them more smoothly. But, to simply tell someone to be smooth is as useless as telling him to be fast. Without knowing exactly how to do it, it's just an empty concept.

I should mention that throughout the text I use the pronoun "he" as a generic for describing riders and "she" for passengers. This is not meant to be sexist in any way. Unfortunately, in the English language we have to choose, and using the "he or she"—or even worse, the singular "they"—options are awkward to read and grammatically incorrect, respectively. So, feel free to substitute he for she and vice versa whenever appropriate.

How to Use It

This book is divided into six sections, which are meant to be read in order—no post-modernist non linearity here. Part 1 covers the physical dynamics of your bike's chassis. I have gone to great lengths to explain the physics involved without requiring any mathematics. Without this understanding, the techniques will not make as much sense, so I encourage you to not skip over it.

Part 2 deals with the psychology of riding. Getting a handle on how your mind relates and reacts to the realities of high-performance motorcycling is just as important as the techniques themselves. By learning to handle fear and control your mind, it will be easier to learn the techniques faster.

In Part 3 you will learn the specific techniques for controlling your motorcycle in a clear and concise format that uses pictures to show not only what to do, but also what it looks like when you do it incorrectly. In teaching the ARCs, I've found that demonstrating both the correct and incorrect way makes the techniques much clearer to the students. To help with this, for many of the techniques I've included drill setup charts so you can practice these skills using the exact same course as my ARCs.

The sample layout is based on a 200-foot-by-300-foot section of clean pavement much like you might find in a large parking lot. The placement of cones is noted in each exercise along with notes for throttle position, braking force, and body position. It's important to make sure the surface is free of dirt and dust, and dry. You can use either a big broom to sweep it or, my preference, a gas-powered leaf blower. Also, it's critical that your tires are up to operating temperature, so I suggest a few minutes of weaving back and forth to scrub some heat into the tires before attempting any of the exercises. Trust me, this is well worth the time.

I highly recommend bringing one or more riding buddies along to practice these drills. Ideally, each will have read the book beforehand, but if not, you can point out in the pictures what they should look for, both positive and negative. This is helpful because riders may think they are doing something correctly when they are not. I also highly recommend using a camcorder to record as much of your practice as possible. When participating in Danny Walker's American Supercamp, I learned the hard way that what I thought I was doing was not what the camera saw. Through its use, however, I was eventually able to get the techniques correct.

Part 4 deals with setting up your bike for high-performance riding. Each of the chapters has useful information, but chapter 15 (Suspension Setup) is the most important and should be considered a prerequisite before doing any of the drills.

Part 5 is about preparing the rider for all this fun. Of particular note is chapter 20 (Riding Gear), which includes

my recommendations based on scientifically testing hundreds of apparel items during my tenure with *Motorcycle Consumer News* as well as almost 20 years of racing.

A plethora of additional resources can be found in the appendix. This includes my recommendations on other books as well as riding schools.

Right Attitude

Although the information in this book is the result of exhaustive clinical testing, there will always be alternative techniques that also work. For example, Larry Pegram, whose form I mercilessly criticize in several chapters of the book, is a much faster racer than I will ever be. Having said that, however, I do believe that by trying each of these techniques, you will find most, if not all, of them to be a great help in improving your riding.

I request that you "try on" the techniques in this book in the same way you might try on a jacket at a store. Remember, just because you try it on, doesn't mean you have to buy it. But the more jackets you try on, the better your chances of finding the one that fits just right. With this attitude you will do well, and don't worry about remembering everything. Remember what you can and it will be enough to work on. When you are ready for more, you can revisit the text. You can't make a wholesale change in every area of your technique in one sitting, so don't try.

Use this book as you would a cookbook. Take it out whenever you forget a specific recipe for good technique. And feel free to mark it up with any personal notes that you find helpful. Like any good cookbook, the more helpful it is, the more it will look like a well-used tool. Of course, there's nothing wrong with having a pristine extra copy on your coffee table for visiting riding buddies.

Finally, before you begin your journey to total control, don't forget to enjoy the process. My personal mantra is "Better living through motorcycling," or as Robert Pirsig put it in *Zen and the Art of Motorcycle Maintenance*, "The real cycle you're working on is a cycle called yourself." By working on your riding skills, not only will you become safer and have more fun, but you will express your true nature through your unique interpretation of the techniques. This is similar to the way a skilled dancer adapts the basic dancing moves to her body's unique structure, effectively putting her "signature" on the movement. When you are fully self-expressed, you become naturally happy and content, so practice these techniques and you will improve your life.

Chapter 1
Traction

Riding a motorcycle is really an exercise in traction management. The purpose of nearly every skill discussed in this book is to maximize available traction and use the limited amounts available to a motorcycle effectively. In order to do that, it's important to first understand what traction is and how it works. This is because riding a motorcycle at speed is really an exercise in traction management. Many things affect traction; some are obvious, many are not.

Tires

Tires are the most critical part of the motorcycle because, in very simple terms, tires are friction providers. They generate friction by complying with the surface of the road to provide a "contact patch." A contact patch occurs when the bottom of a tire flattens as it contacts the road, forming a somewhat elliptical pattern. Larger and softer tires provide a larger contact patch and greater friction. The rubber on a tire also conforms to the small peaks and valleys of the road's surface, creating a series of microscopic interlocking "teeth" that hold the motorcycle to the road.

There are several factors affecting the contact patch and, ultimately, traction. Tire pressure determines how much the tire will flatten out as it contacts the road. Wide, soft tires with low air pressure generate bigger

contact patches and greater friction than narrow, hard tires with high air pressure. In some forms of competition like observed trials and drag racing, tires are inflated to very low pressures to maximize the size of the contact patch and traction.

The problem with running a low-pressure tire is that the load capacity of the tire is reduced, and the internal friction of the tire is increased, generating heat. This causes the tire temperature to rise, sometimes to dangerous levels. Road racers use small increases in tire pressure, as little as a half a pound at a time, to adjust the temperature of a tire. For street riding, it is very important not to stray too far from the manufacturers' recommended tire pressures as tires have been designed to provide the correct amount of contact patch and flexing at a given load and pressure.

The temperature of a tire also helps determine the amount of traction it will provide. As a tire gets hotter, the rubber becomes more compliant and has a greater ability to interlock with the tarmac, providing greater traction. This increased traction continues until the rubber exceeds its design temperature and begins to degrade. At this point, the tire may begin to leach oil, or its tread may sep-

The road surface has a huge impact on your available traction, and it is always changing with weather, temperature, debris, etc. You don't want to push the bike too hard if you aren't totally sure about the condition of the surface on that day.

arate from the carcass, or worse yet, both conditions may occur simultaneously. How many times have you heard a racer in an interview say his tires got "greasy" or "blistered?" What he's really saying is that his tires got too hot.

Conversely, when tires are cold, the rubber becomes hard and doesn't conform to the peaks and valleys of the road surface as well as when the tires are warm, significantly reducing grip. This is especially true of race compound tires. Pushing too hard on cold tires has caused me and nearly every racer I know to crash. It's also been responsible for a lot of crashes on the street, especially when street bikes are equipped with DOT race tires, which are race-compound tires that have been cut with a tread so that they are approved by the Department of Transportation for street use.

Tires range in compound from super-sticky "qualifying" race tires to rock-like touring tires that provide extra-long life. What is not obvious, however, is that the compound and compliance of a tire changes with time. As tires are heated and cooled from riding and parking, they become harder. Racers refer to this process as a "heat cycle," and it is especially pronounced with soft racing tires. Tires also become harder by just sitting in a warehouse or garage. This is something to keep in mind when those cheap, closeout tires in the magazine ads tempt you. Those tires may be fine, but then again they may have sat in a warehouse for so long that they've practically turned to stone.

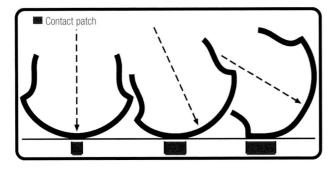

Modern-day tires use a "multi-arc profile" (the tread profile varies across the tire) design in an attempt to get the quick steering of a narrower tire while upright and the higher traction of a wider tire at full lean. Notice how the contact patch grows as the bike leans over.

Tire construction varies greatly depending on its purpose. DOT-approved racing tires (left) are designed to maximize friction in dry conditions by having very little tread, especially on the edges. They act similar to a slick at full lean but must get very hot to work properly, which is why they don't make good street tires. In order to maximize traction in wet conditions, racing "rain slicks" (middle) use extremely soft rubber compounds and lots of tread to help channel water and dirt away from the contact patch. If used in dry conditions the soft rubber would burn up very quickly and start to chunk off. A cruiser tire (right), by comparison, also uses lots of tread groves to channel water away but uses a harder rubber compound that lasts longer and sticks better at the colder tire temperatures associated with cruising. Photo courtesy of Avon.

The profile of a tire determines how much traction will be available at specific lean angles. For instance, a tire with a rounded profile will have relatively equal amounts of traction at any lean angle. On the other hand, a tire with a more triangular profile will have less traction when it is on the pointy part of the tire during acceleration, but more traction in the corners when it is at full lean.

One bad thing about motorcycle tires is they do not wear evenly across the surface. If you ride primarily on highways, you will wear out the center of the tires faster than the edges. If you ride on the track or aggressively in the twisties, you will wear out the tires' edges first. Because of this uneven wear, a tire's profile changes over time, adversely affecting traction and handling.

If traction were the only consideration in rating tires, the best tires would be the biggest ones. Unfortunately, the size of the tires affects not only traction, but handling as well. As you put larger tires on a motorcycle, the traction will increase. However, the ease of steering will decrease. The correct tire sizes provide the best compromise between traction and handling. Keep in mind that the tire size that provides the best handling isn't always the same size as the stock size. Sometimes manufacturers mount rear tires that are too wide for stylistic reasons—fat rear tires look cool. For example, when Triumph revamped its Daytona 955 in 2002, it switched from a 190-mm wide rear tire to a narrower 180-mm rear tire because the narrower tire provided more agile handling. Unfortunately, customers wanted the look of a fatter rear tire, and for 2003 Triumph sacrificed handling and switched back to a 190-mm rear tire. And Triumph isn't the only culprit.

Road Conditions

The condition of the road is just as important as the tires when determining the amount of traction. Surface hazards like rain, dust, oil, or painted lines can drastically reduce traction. When encountering such obstacles, some tires are more forgiving than others. Generally, touring and cruiser tires have more, larger, and deeper grooves than sport tires. The grooves are designed to channel water, oil, and dirt away from the contact patch. Some DOT-labeled racing tires have no tread on the outside edges, effectively making them slicks at full lean.

It is also important to note that traction varies depending on the type of pavement used on a road's surface. Asphalt generally provides better traction than concrete, but that can change depending on the surface texture. For example, I've ridden on polished concrete that was slipperier than dirt. I've also raced on "grated"

Riding a motorcycle at speed requires excellent traction management skills. Amazingly, only a few square inches of rubber (contact patch) are keeping you and the bike upright.

concrete that stuck like glue but wore out tires at twice the rate of asphalt.

Suspension

The condition, quality, and tuning of your suspension have a profound impact on the available traction. In fact, the suspension system's most important job isn't isolating you from the bumps in the road, it's keeping the tires firmly on the tarmac by applying even pressure at all times. If there is too little pressure, the friction coefficient will be insufficient to maintain traction. Conversely, if there is too much pressure, the rubber can tear away from the tire causing a skid.

If the suspension is improperly maintained or tuned (see chapter 15), the wheels will move up and down too fast or slow to keep steady pressure on the constantly changing road surface. This can easily lead to a loss of contact with the pavement. No matter how good your tires are, if they don't touch the pavement, they won't provide any grip.

Traction Pizza

Not only must you be concerned about the amount of traction available, you must also be able to manage it well. In order to understand this concept better, imagine that traction is a sliced pizza. Let's say that we have ten slices of available traction in our pizza. If you let Mr. Cornering have all ten pieces you will have none left for Mr. Acceleration and Ms. Braking. That might be okay assuming you don't need Ms. Braking's services. Of course, if you give eight slices of pizza to Mr. Cornering and attempt to have Ms. Braking stop you in a hurry you may run out of pizza and fall. The moral of the story is to always keep some spare pizza for any unexpected guests.

In reality, things are a bit more complex than divvying up one 10-piece pizza. Each tire must share its pizza with the other tire, and the tires can steal slices from each other. However, by doing so, some of the toppings may fall off, reducing the total amount of pizza available.

Braking

Tires generally produce more grip as the load on them increases. This is why the front brake is so important, especially on a sportbike. The weight carried by the front wheel increases as you decelerate. Shorter wheelbases and higher centers of gravity make this effect more pronounced. Because the weight carried by the front wheel increases under braking, more front brake can be used than would be possible without the weight transfer. As a result, the rear brake on most sportbikes becomes

While grooves in a tire reduce the total surface area of rubber that is in contact with the road, they perform the important function of channeling water away from the contact patch, thus helping to prevent hydroplaning.

useless under hard braking as the rear wheel lightly skims over—or even lifts completely off—the ground.

Cornering

Things get a little more complicated when cornering is involved. During hard turns, Mr. Cornering demands a large share of the pizza. If you need to accelerate or decelerate quickly, you must make sure Mr. Cornering has left enough pizza to share with Mr. Acceleration or Ms. Braking or you will run out of pizza, which of course means you will soon become intimate with Ms. Pavement.

It's actually possible to lose control of the front end of the bike when taking a corner. This can occur when you suddenly close the throttle, perhaps as a result of fear. As you close the throttle, the engine acts as a brake (this is called compression braking), slowing the rear wheel, which causes the motorcycle to pitch forward. The front wheel now has more weight pressing down on it. Normally that would provide increased traction, but in this situation, the front wheel must also support a larger portion of the cornering load. Unfortunately, the increase in traction from the greater pressure is less than the additional cornering load put on the tire. This results in a net loss of traction, which can cause the front tire to wash out. Put another way, the front tire's appetite becomes bigger than the amount of pizza available. Too much trail braking (see chapter 11) has a similar effect.

Accelerating

When you accelerate, weight is transferred from the front wheel to the rear one. If the weight transfers quickly enough, the front wheelies off the ground as witnessed in many forms of motorsports.

When accelerating out of a corner (especially a slower one) with a powerful sportbike, it is easy to use the throttle to ask for more pizza than is available. When this happens, the rear wheel "spins up," and the motorcycle begins to rotate in the yaw-axis. The natural survival response is to stop this occurrence by closing the throttle. Unfortunately, although this action will restore traction to the sliding rear tire, it will do it so rapidly that it may result in the rider being thrown over the "high side" of the motorcycle. High siding is basically the conversion of forward speed to rotational speed, which acts like a catapult and launches the rider. In other words, high siding is the quickest way to meet what Gonzo journalist Hunter S. Thompson calls Mr. "Sausage Creature."

Lean Angle

Lean angle also affects grip, but not for the reasons you might think. At higher lean angles, motorcycle suspension becomes less efficient because the moving parts are no longer perpendicular to the forces being applied to them. In essence, the spring rates become progressively stiffer, and the sideways forces cause sliding parts to flex against one another causing additional friction. To counter these inefficiencies, motorcycle engineers design in a "tuned" amount of chassis and tire flex. This is helpful because at maximum lean the frame and tire sidewalls are at a better angle to absorb bumps in the road than the suspension system. Unfortunately, despite the engineers' best efforts, the total pizza available still gets slightly smaller as lean angles increase.

The composite center of gravity, or CG, of the rider and the bike also affects lean angle. The composite CG is the combination of the rider's CG and the bike's CG. The farther the rider's CG is to the inside of the turn, the smaller the lean angle needed for a given radius and speed. This is why racers hang off in the turns. Basically, riders can increase traction by reducing the bike's lean angle. And they can reduce the lean angle by repositioning the CG (see chapter 12) and reducing the amount of time spent at full lean (see chapter 8).

Traction Management

As you can see, there are many things that affect traction. Learning to manage them all might sound overwhelming at first. However, by reading the following chapters, you can learn exactly what you need to know, without being bogged down by overly sophisticated academic theories. Just stay focused on each of the drills as you do them, and traction will take care of itself.

Chapter 2
Steering

Because motorcycles are single-track vehicles, they lack static balance and must lean to turn. Steering a motorcycle is a much more complex process than steering a multi-track vehicle like an automobile because of this. In order to understand how to steer a motorcycle, you first need to understand steering geometry.

Rake and Trail

You've probably read magazine articles that give the "rake" and "trail" measurements of the latest model, but what do these numbers really mean?

Rake and trail are interrelated values that define the amount of caster of the front wheel. To understand caster, look at any shopping cart. Or, if you're sitting in an office chair reading this book, take a look at the wheels on the chair. You'll notice that the steering axis of each wheel is mounted off-center from the wheel axle. No matter how you push the shopping cart or office chair, the wheel always follows the steering axis of the wheel. This effect is called caster.

Countersteering is steering the bars in the opposite direction of the turn to get the bike to lean over. However, in slower turns that doesn't necessarily mean the front wheel will be steered past the bike's centerline, as can be seen in this photo.

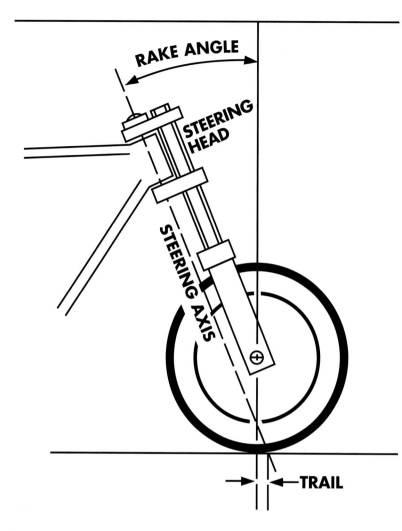

RAKE ANGLE

STEERING HEAD

STEERING AXIS

TRAIL

If you draw an imaginary line through the steering axis, it will end up at a spot in front of the tire's contact patch. The distance between that point and the center of the contact patch is the trail. You can also imagine the center of the contact patch as a vertical line drawn through the front axle. Trail is what makes the wheel want to re-center itself whenever it is turned. Stability increases and steering slows and becomes more difficult as trail is added.

Rake and trail determine the amount of caster a motorcycle has. Rake is the angle from vertical of the steering axis measured in degrees. Trail is a linear measurement. If you could extend the steering axis from the steering head of the frame down to the ground and then drop a plumb line from the front axle, the distance between the point the line from the steering axis intersected the ground and the point the plumb line touched the ground would be the trail in millimeters.

Think of trail as a "correcting wrench" that steers the tire back in the direction of travel. The tire always wants to follow behind the steering axis in the same way crooked wheels straighten out as soon as you push a shopping cart forward. More trail has the same effect as a longer wrench handle. In other words, when the wheel gets out of line, the trail wrenches it back in line.

Given the same triple-clamp offset, the trail is positively correlated to the rake. In other words, the more rake you have, the more trail exists. Generally speaking, sportbikes and dirt bikes have steeper rakes and shorter trails for quick maneuvering, while tourers and cruisers have greater amounts of rake and trail to promote straight-line stability.

Counter Steering vs. Body Steering

As long as I have been riding, a debate has raged between proponents of countersteering and proponents of rider lean, or body steering. It has been my experience that you can indeed make fine course corrections using only rider weight shifts while in the middle of a turn. However, rider weight shifts are incapable of resulting in rapid directional changes. This was scientifically proven with Keith Code's "No B.S. Bike Trainer." The trainer utilized a second set of handlebars rigidly affixed to the frame along with a throttle. Riders found it was impossible to make quick or accurate steering inputs by shifting only their body weight. Body steering may make a fine supplemental steering technique, but it can never be the primary force for directional changes.

How Countersteering Works

Simply put, countersteering is applying pressure to the inside handlebar in the direction of the intended turn and pushing forward. By "inside" handlebar, I mean the bar that's on the same side as the side to which you are turning. At first, this may seem counter-intuitive as you are turning the front wheel of the bike in the direction opposite of where you want to travel. By steering the wheel in the opposite direction, the bike wants to tip to the inside. This is a result of the centrifugal force created by the turning.

For a given speed, rider position and bike setup are the two primary factors affecting a bike's turning ability.

Many people assume the term countersteering means that the wheel must cross the bike's centerline for countersteering to happen. Although the wheel does indeed cross the center and point the opposite way when initiating a turn from an upright position, in slow, tight corners with a larger steering angle, the wheel will likely never cross the center.

Automobiles (or sidecars or trikes) don't fall over when they are steered into a turn because they are multi-tracked. The second "track" of wheels that is located toward the outside of the vehicle's center of gravity counters the effects of centrifugal force by transferring weight laterally to the outside wheels. When cornering hard in a car, you can feel the effect of centrifugal force as the vehicle tries to pull your body to the inside of the turn while your body tries to go straight.

It should be noted that too much centrifugal force will eventually cause a vehicle to flip over as sometimes happens with tall, narrow sport utility vehicles. Of

course, that's assuming the SUV has enough traction to keep from sliding. Conversely, a motorcycle has no outside wheel to support the lateral weight transfer caused by the centrifugal force so it falls in the opposite direction of the steering.

Riding a motorcycle is a balancing act. When you lean over, gravity tries to pull the bike into the ground. At the same time, centrifugal force tries to throw you to the outside of the turn. By moving your body weight to the inside of the turn, as racers do when they "hang off," you're helping gravity do its job. Your body shift reduces the amount of countersteering force needed to maintain a given line. This is why top racers make it look so easy going around turns. It *is* easy on their bodies, because they're giving the gravitational force a longer "lever" to counter the effects of centrifugal inertia.

As you've learned, countersteering the motorcycle causes it to lean and ultimately turn. The harder you push on the inside bar, the faster the motorcycle will

If you can position your body farther down and closer to the inside of the turn, the bike will need less lean angle to negotiate the turn. This picture was taken during a rain race at Summit Point where three of us were taking a similar arc at a similar speed. Notice how my bike, number 311, needs less lean angle than the other two bikes. This is because I moved my center of gravity closer to the inside of the turn. This allows for an earlier and harder application of throttle at the exit. By looking farther into the turn, I was also in a better position to maximize my arc, formulate my exit strategy, and prepare myself for any danger ahead.

lean; the longer you hold pressure, the farther it will lean. When you get to the intended lean angle, you simply release some or all of the pressure on the bar, and the bike will hold a particular radius around the turn. After reaching your intended lean angle, the self-correcting (castering) effect of the trail and gyroscopic precession keep the bike on the intended line. At this point, the physics get a little more complicated.

Gyroscopic Precession

As a motorcycle travels down the road, it actually moves in a nearly undetectable low-amplitude weave, even when the rider thinks it is going straight. This is due to a multitude of factors like uneven pavement and tire profiles, the elastic properties of tire rubber, and the constantly changing weight distribution from rider and suspension movements.

When this happens, the bike begins to fall to one side, and a phenomenon known as gyroscopic precession causes the wheel to turn into the direction of the fall. At this point, our old friend centrifugal force pushes the motorcycle in the opposite direction. This process is repeated over and over, creating the low-amplitude weave.

Working in tandem with gyroscopic precession is gyroscopic momentum, which is caused by the motorcycle's spinning wheels. To understand these phenomena, you will need to perform a simple experiment. Hold a bicycle wheel by the axle and have a partner spin the wheel so that the top moves away from you. Now try to steer the wheel. Notice how it resists your input and attempts to maintain its plane of rotation. Next hold your arms straight out in front of you and have your partner spin the wheel again. This time, lean the wheel as if it is entering a curve. Notice that the wheel tends to turn into the direction of lean. This turning effect is gyroscopic precession.

The gyroscopic momentum increases with wheel weight, wider weight distribution, and rotational speed. This is the reason steering becomes more difficult as the bike goes faster and the reason why racers buy lightweight wheels to improve cornering. On the plus side, increased wheel speed improves chassis stability, which is why you can take your hands off the bars at highway speeds without falling over, but cannot do this at super-slow parking-lot speeds.

Steering Technique

It is my ardent belief that when cornering, you should use only your inside arm to steer. This includes both pushing and pulling when appropriate. I recommend this because it's extremely difficult for both arms to put reverse inputs into opposite ends of the bars in precise unison while simultaneously allowing enough "give" in the steering for gyroscopic precession to do its thing.

That advice may sound strange, but in my Advanced Riding Clinics the single biggest hindrance my students have in holding a tight line is that both arms are fighting for control of the steering. The problem is easy to spot by looking at how tense riders' arms get as they stiffen and rise away from the gas tank.

Although I originally came up with this theory while watching a video of my students in action, I proved its validity the hard way while participating in one of Freddie Spencer's High-Performance Riding Schools. As I approached a turn that was giving me problems, one that had me almost running off the outside, I decided to test my hypothesis and just let my inside arm do all the work. And, boy, did it ever work. In fact, initiating the turn at the exact same position on the track, even with substantially less effort on the bars, I turned so much quicker that I ran off the *inside* of the track and actually crashed. *Sorry again, Freddie.* I was obviously on to something.

Ever since I incorporated the "steering with only the inside arm" technique into the curriculum, my students have been making amazing breakthroughs. As soon as the students stop arm-wrestling with themselves for control of the handlebars, their bikes become much more efficient turning machines.

Freed from the conflicting inputs of the two arms, the bike is allowed to do what it was engineered to do, turning smoother and much quicker at the given speed. In fact, the moment the student releases pressure from the outside arm, the bike immediately wants to run off the inside of the course. Many students end up making a dramatic bobble to keep from running off the inside as they compensate for the newfound steering ability. As they practice the technique and become more proficient, students learn to use the throttle to help counter lean angle by increasing or decreasing speed. In addition, their lines become smooth, and their riding begins to appear effortless. Eventually, they enter the "Zone" we talk about later in this book.

I have actually had professional car racers tell me they do a similar thing when racing in the rain. By having one hand dominate the steering, they can allow the vehicle to do whatever self-corrective "wiggling" it needs to do as it struggles for traction in the wet.

To exit the corner, simply reverse the process and countersteer in the opposite direction. For example, to exit a right-handed corner, pull on the right grip or push on the left grip. You'll find that the bike will stand up. The same effect can be produced by accelerating because you are creating additional centrifugal force to prop you up. Generally speaking, a combination of the two will work best.

As you have learned, there are many forces at work during the steering process. Fortunately, many of them take care of themselves, just like the wheels on that shopping cart. The most important thing to remember about steering is that the more skillfully you use your body's weight as a lever, the less force you will need to apply to the controls, and the more precise your steering will become. The techniques in this book are designed to teach you exactly that.

Chapter 3
Suspension

I t is my belief that no real discussion of proper riding technique can take place without first understanding the basics of suspension dynamics. Your bike's suspension system has a profound effect on both traction and handling. Every movement you make on a motorcycle affects your suspension, and what happens to your suspension happens to you. Enhanced control, better traction, and more compliance translate into improved safety, more comfort, and increased affinity for street riding. On top of all of that, you'll enjoy lower lap times on the track. Let's take a theoretical look at what suspension is and how it works.

Why Suspension?

Why do we need suspension in the first place? After all, go-carts move pretty fast with no suspension at all, other than tire and chassis flex. When trying to answer this, it's important to remember that go-carts travel over fairly smooth surfaces while motorcycles encounter bumps. This is where suspension makes a difference. The purpose of the suspension is threefold: to minimize harshness, maximize traction, and maximize control. The ideal setup is determined by a number of factors, including the type of riding (racing or street, for example) and personal preference (some like it stiffer, some like it plusher).

Imagine the perfect ride produced by the perfect suspension. It's firm with good resistance to bottoming and great "feel" for the road, yet it is plush and comfortable at the same time. Every type of rider can relate to this ideal setup—firmness for that feeling of control, and plushness because no one likes getting beat up while riding. The terms "firmness" and "plushness" seem mutually exclusive, but are they? Is this type of ride stiff or is it soft? Well, the answer is both— firm to eliminate excessive dive and control bottoming, and plush on the square edge bumps. Although it doesn't sound logical, firmness and plushness don't have to be mutually exclusive. Let's find out just how the perfect ride can be achieved.

Forces

There are three distinct types of forces involved in suspension action: spring, damping, and frictional. There are also forces created by acceleration of the masses

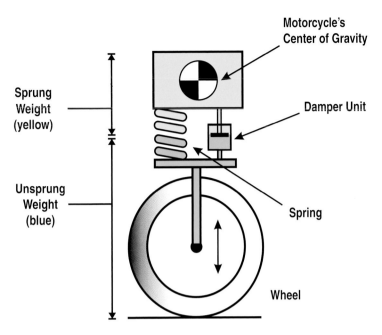

Motorcycle's Center of Gravity

Damper Unit

Sprung Weight (yellow)

Spring

Unsprung Weight (blue)

Wheel

Front and rear motorcycle suspension systems have the same basic components.

(component weight) involved, but they will be ignored for the purpose of this discussion.

The first type of force is spring force. The key point to remember about spring force is that it is dependent only on its position regarding the overall travel of the suspension. It is not affected by how fast the suspension is compressing or rebounding.

Damping force is caused when liquids are forced through some type of restriction. The key point to remember about damping is that the amount of damping force is dependent on fluid movement. The velocity of the oil moving through the damping cartridge, or washer stack, creates the damping force. This also means a shock creates no damping force unless there is movement of the damper unit during compression or rebound. Damping is not affected by bike movement or bike speed, only by vertical wheel velocity.

The third type of force is frictional force. Frictional force depends on the perpendicular load on the surfaces in question and the materials involved, including lubrication, if any. The higher the load, the greater the friction between the inner tube and the bushings and the seals attached to the outer fork tube.

The other factor concerning friction is whether there is movement between the surfaces. These two

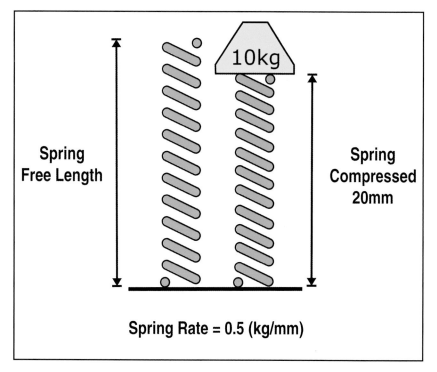

Spring Free Length

10kg

Spring Compressed 20mm

Spring Rate = 0.5 (kg/mm)

Spring rate can be found by measuring the force needed to compress it, divided by how far it travels or displaces.

conditions are known as "static friction" (or "stiction"), and "dynamic friction." Stiction is created when there is no movement between the surfaces; dynamic friction is created when there is movement. Stiction can be readily felt in front forks when you push down on the handlebars. The breakaway resistance, or stiction, is higher than the friction before there is movement. For now we only need to note that stiction is always higher than dynamic friction.

In some cases, frictional forces can be the biggest suspension problem, larger than the damping and spring forces combined. Low-friction materials, better surface finishes, more sophisticated lubricants, and better designs can minimize friction. Suffice it to say, as far as frictional forces are concerned, less is always better.

Energy

Forces are important, but it's essential to understand the larger picture: energy. Springs store energy when they're compressed. They release energy when they recoil. Damping, on the other hand, turns mechanical energy into heat and then transfers it to the air. Friction also turns mechanical energy into heat, but its characteristics are quite different from damping forces. Why is this knowledge of energy important? There are a

number of reasons. First, riders often get very concerned when their shocks get hot. Once you understand that, on an energy level, a damper's job is to turn mechanical energy into heat, you realize it's not a problem for the shocks to get hot. However, shock fade, a condition where the shock loses its damping, is undesirable. A well-designed shock absorber with high-quality fluid can get hot and still not fade perceptibly.

An understanding of energy helps to greatly simplify the subject of suspension. When a tire comes in contact with a bump, the suspension compresses. As it does, the spring stores some of the energy, while the damper turns some of the remaining energy into heat. The suspension slows down, stops compressing, changes direction, and starts extending or rebounding. The spring releases energy, and the damper applies rebound damping, once again turning mechanical energy into heat. If everything goes perfectly, the center of gravity of the motorcycle follows a straight line, with the wheel moving up and down beneath it. Perfect contact is maintained with the road surface. That's how it's supposed to work, but it's easier said than done.

A suspended motorcycle system is illustrated in figure 1. Note that the center of gravity is separated from the wheel by the spring and the damping unit. Each of these components has mass or weight. Everything above the spring is considered to be "sprung mass," and everything below the spring is considered to be "unsprung mass." Half the spring is sprung, and half is unsprung. The portions of the damper attached to the sprung mass are considered sprung, and the portions attached to the unsprung mass are unsprung. When going over a series of bumps on that "perfect ride," the center of gravity of the sprung mass traces a straight line as the wheel and unsprung mass move up and down, maintaining contact with the road surface and, therefore, providing traction.

Springs

Everyone knows what a spring is, but few understand exactly how it works or know the differences between various types of springs. Let's begin by defining what spring rate and preload really are. Spring rate is the "stiffness" of the spring, measured in kilograms per millimeter or pounds per inch. One of the ways to test spring rate is to first measure the spring's free, or uninstalled, length. Then put some weight on it and measure the amount it compresses as shown in figure 2. By placing increasingly heavier weights on the spring and measuring how much the spring compresses, a graph comparing force to displacement can be plotted.

Spring rate is defined as the change in force divided by the change in displacement. In algebraic terms, that's spring rate (K) = (change in force)/(change in displacement).

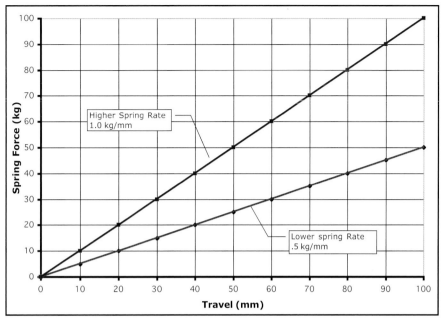

The blue straight-rate spring requires 5 kg of force to compress it 10mm throughout its entire range. The red spring is twice as stiff requiring 10 kg to compress it 10mm.

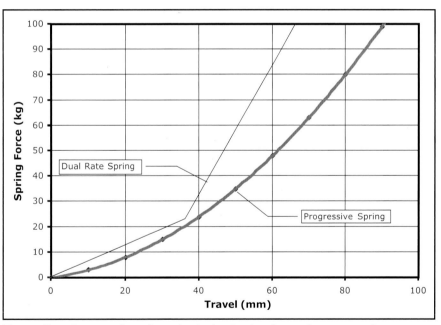

Two other types of springs include dual-rate and progressive springs. Progressive springs gradually increase force over a given distance of travel while dual-rate springs act like two separate springs combined into one coil.

What this means is that the slope created when plotting the force in relation to the displacement is the spring rate.

A straight-rate spring (figure 3) maintains a constant rate throughout its travel and is very common

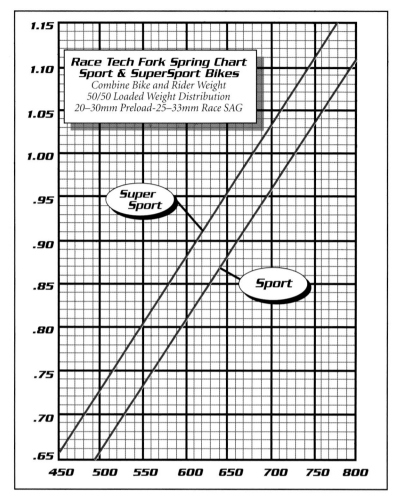

Use this chart to determine what rate fork springs you should have in your bike for optimum handling. It works with any brand of fork spring. Courtesy of Race Tech.

in racing applications. A progressive or dual rate spring (figure 4), by contrast, changes the amount of force in relation to the position of travel.

During installation, a spring gets compressed a small amount. This compression is referred to as preload length, or simply "preload." Preload is the distance the spring is compressed compared to its free length when installed. This distance is measured in millimeters or inches. All motorcycles with sprung suspensions have preload. This is true even for the bikes that don't have preload adjusters. Forks that do have external preload adjustment have spring preload even when set at the minimum adjustment. It is incorrect to assume the fork has no preload if the adjuster is backed out all the way. For example, the preload may range from 20 to 35 millimeters with the adjuster having only 15

millimeters to travel. It is important to note that all types of forks can have the preload adjusted internally by changing spring spacer length, although sometimes this requires special spacers.

The preload force, which is different from the preload length, is the initial force the spring exerts on the end of the fork tube with the fork fully extended. For a particular spring, increasing the amount of preload (spacer length) will increase the preload force.

When you tighten the adjusting collar on a shock or increase the preload length by tightening the adjusters or changing the spacer length on forks, you are indeed increasing the initial force exerted by the springs. This decreases the spring sag, keeping the bike from "sagging" closer to the ground. Spring sag is the amount the springs compress between fully topped out and fully loaded with the rider on board in riding position. It does not, however, increase the spring rate. For example, on front forks you can achieve a particular static sag with a spring that is too light if you use a lot of preload, or displacement. You can also achieve that same sag with a spring that is too heavy, using very little or no preload.

The quality of the ride will suffer when a spring is either too soft or too stiff. The spring with a rate that's too soft will dive and bottom easily because the spring doesn't provide enough additional force as it gets deeper into the travel. On the other hand, the spring with a very stiff rate will feel harsh, as if it had hit a wall or a stiff spot in its travel.

By taking a few measurements, you can see if your spring rates are in the ballpark (figure 5). Most street bikes are set up with fork springs that are too soft for aggressive riding even on the street. Racers generally use higher spring rates with less preload than street riders. However, personal preference, conditions, and type of riding (street or racing) come into play when setting up suspension. Don't make the mistake of trying to set up your street bike like a racer, or it will try to shake your tooth fillings out on bumpy roads. When in doubt, consult a good suspension tuner.

To conclude, static sag for a particular bike and rider combination is determined by spring rate and preload only. Springs are position-sensitive and are affected by where they are in the travel of the suspension, not by how fast they are being compressed. Damping settings are dynamic forces, meaning that they only occur when there is vertical suspension movement. Damping settings do not affect static sag, which is measured when there is no suspension movement.

I want to add a couple of final thoughts about air pressure and oil level. On models with air valves built into the fork caps, the addition of air in the forks has a huge effect on both sag and harshness. I don't recommend the use of air as a tuning variable because harshness generally increases significantly for the relatively small benefit in bottoming resistance. Adding air is almost like adding spring preload instead of spring rate. For example, the use of additional air pressure is quite effective on touring bikes for temporarily changing the load-carrying capacity for riding two-up. It's not a great solution, but on a bike that is not designed for high-performance riding like a touring bike, it will do the trick. Changes in oil level affect the total spring force, but the effect is negligible in the first half of the travel. The effect is felt in the second half of the stroke as the fork reaches the bottom of the stroke; therefore, it does not affect sag.

Rebound Damping

When it comes to overall ride and handling characteristics, many professional tuners consider damping to be the most critical factor. It's a complex subject, so I'll start with the basics. Damping is viscous friction. It turns mechanical energy into heat and is sensitive only to velocity, not to suspension stroke position. This is fundamentally different from a spring, which stores energy and is only sensitive to position in the stroke. Damping in modern motorcycle suspension components is accomplished in different ways, but always involves a fluid. The configuration can be as simple as shoving oil through a hole, as with old-style damping rod forks, or can be as sophisticated as a multi-stage bending shim-stack configuration in combination with an internally or externally adjustable bleed circuit. There are two primary types of damping: compression damping and rebound damping.

Compression damping, or "bump damping," occurs when the wheel contacts a bump and compresses the suspension. Rebound, or "tension damping," occurs when the spring forces the shock or forks to extend, coming back toward the ground. Most current sportbikes have external adjustments for both compression and rebound damping as well as for spring

Suspension isn't only about handling changes in the road surface. It must also deal with weight transfers caused by accelerating, braking, and rider movement. Even with enviably smooth technique, Suzuki's Matt Mladin all but bottoms the forks under braking.

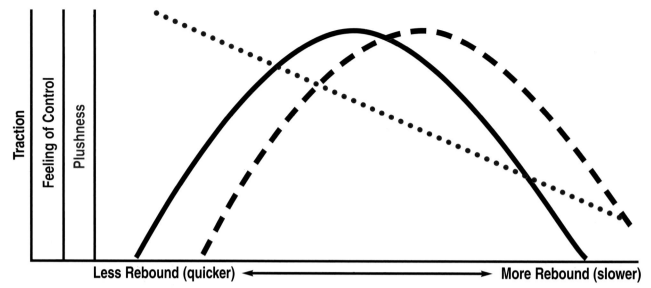

Less Rebound (quicker) ⟵——————————⟶ **More Rebound (slower)**

No matter where you adjust the rebound setting, you'll always be faced with a compromise between traction, control, and plushness.

preload. A fork uses a screw adjustment located atop the leg for rebound damping. This is not to be confused with the surrounding spring preload adjuster. There is another screw on the bottom near the axle for compression damping. On rear shocks, the adjuster on the reservoir is for compression, and the one on the shaft eyelet is for rebound damping. These adjusters, often referred to as "clickers," have their limits and typically affect only a small portion of the entire damping range. In other words, even if you have external adjustment capabilities, that doesn't make up for poor internal valve design. External damping adjustments can never make up for extremely worn out dampers. If your bike is wallowing like a 1963 Cadillac with blown shocks, you might want to do some suspension rebuilding or replacement before you spend the rest of your life playing with the adjusting clickers.

Let's take a closer look at rebound damping. Changes in rebound damping affect traction. If you look at figure 6, you'll see that all of these factors are plotted. There are no numbers on the Y-axis because these are largely subjective quantities. In other words, the discussion is about the ride "feel." You will notice that traction starts at very light, or quick, rebound-damping settings, increases to a maximum, and decreases again. Why does this happen? At very light rebound settings, the chassis is uncontrolled. When the wheel hits a bump, the shock is compressed. The shock then rebounds downward without any control. In

fact, it extends too far because the sprung weight of the chassis is moving upward. This upward movement of the chassis causes the wheel to be pulled off the ground, thereby losing traction.

Look at the traction-versus-rebound-damping curve (figure 6). Note that at a high rebound-damping setting, or slow rebound, traction will suffer. The suspension compresses as it hits a bump. As you travel up the bump and reach the top, the suspension attempts to follow the surface of the road back down the other side. The wheel is unable to follow the road surface, simply because it can't respond fast enough to maintain traction. When this becomes excessive, it is referred to as "packing" because the suspension is packed into a shorter travel area. Maximum traction occurs somewhere between these two rebound-damping extremes.

Your own riding experience may have shown you that when rebound damping is very light, the feeling of control is minimized. The bike feels "loose" and bouncy. As you increase rebound damping, the feeling of control increases as the chassis doesn't move around nearly as much, and the bike feels more "planted" and stable. When rebound damping is set to higher settings, meaning there's a lot of damping and the suspension rebounds slowly, traction is poor, and the feeling of control suffers. Once again, somewhere between the two extremes, the feeling of control is maximized.

There is a trade-off between maximum traction and control. Notice that maximum traction does not necessarily occur at the same damping setting that yields a maximum feeling of control. Herein lies a common problem. Quite often riders have mistaken ideas about how much damping should be used. They think the faster they are, or the faster they want to be, the more damping they need. Nothing could be further from the truth. In fact, after reaching a certain level of increased rebound damping, traction, control, and ride quality, or "plushness," are all sacrificed. Even with rebound-damping settings falling between these two extremes, a trade-off still exists.

I will offer one word of caution. During testing, the only way you will ever know if you have less traction for a specific suspension setting is if you are at the limit of traction. This is a very delicate position for a rider. Without being at this limit, the point at which the tires begin to slide, you can't feel the difference in traction between one setting and another. As you can imagine, it is very easy to slide too far and crash if you're not careful when riding on the edge of traction, even for experienced riders. The trick in testing is to be aware of this relationship and plan your evaluation accordingly.

The job of both the suspension engineer and suspension tuner is to make these two peaks, the traction and the feeling of control, as close to the same point as possible. This is done by reshaping the damping curve inside the forks or shock. This requires an understanding of high- and low-speed damping as well as valving piston design. The relationship among damping, spring forces, weight bias, and all the other factors that make a bike handle is also important. Although this complexity may seem overwhelming, making adjustments one at a time or, literally, one click at a time, helps.

Another ride quantity that is affected by rebound damping is plushness. At very light rebound damping, the wheel moves very quickly, and the ride quality is plush or mushy. As rebound damping increases, there is more and more resistance to movement. At maximum damping, the wheel is packing so much that the chassis is sucked down in its travel and cannot recover for the next bump. When you hit the next bump, the suspension has to overcome the added spring force due to this compression, or packing. The result is a jolt to the chassis upon impact.

Compression Damping

Compression damping is one of the most critical, yet easily misunderstood, components of suspension tuning. Understanding how compression damping affects ride quality will go a long way toward demystifying the "witches' brew" of how motorcycle suspension works.

A fundamental difference exists between compression and rebound velocity profiles. Compression

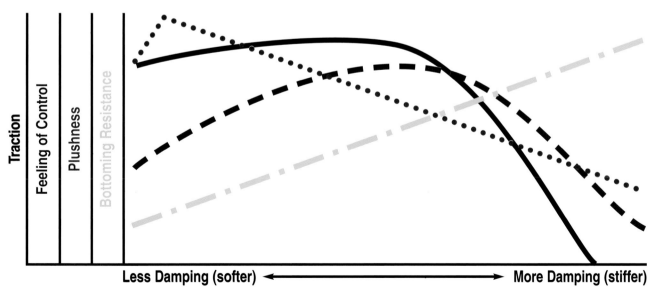

FIGURE 7: COMPRESSION DAMPING ADJUSTMENT RANGE

Less Damping (softer) ← → More Damping (stiffer)

Like all suspension settings, compression damping is a system of trade-offs. Depending on what kind of riding you do, pick the best compromise for what's most important.

Finding the best suspension settings can completely transform a motorcycle's handling.

velocity is determined by the bump encountered, while rebound velocity is caused primarily by spring force. This means that for proper compression damping, the shape of the bump is far more important than its size. A square-edged bump results in extremely high shaft velocities, while a bump with a gradual slope causes lower velocities. Granted, when you hit a bump at twice the bike speed, the shaft velocity also increases, but the shape of the bump is the critical factor.

In the past, many considered compression damping a necessary evil. They assumed less was better. This stems from the limitations of old-style damping rod forks, or orifice-style damping, which can be simultaneously too harsh and too mushy. This is due in part to how much fluid can be forced through any

given sized hole at different velocities. With the advent of cartridge-type forks found on most sportbikes and Emulators (Race Tech's damping control valves for damping rod forks), the ability to control the shape of the damping curve has changed dramatically.

To study the effects of altering compression damping settings, it's important to look at damping as a whole. For now, ignore the shape of the damping curve. The amount of compression damping affects traction, plushness, bottoming resistance, and dynamic dive. Consider bottoming resistance. Referring to figure 7, notice that the more compression damping there is, the more resistance there is to bottoming. It may seem obvious, but you need to have the right amount of compression damping, not too much or too little. The compression damping force is added to the spring forces to help resist bottoming. At the same time that bottoming resistance increases, the feeling of plushness decreases. On the flip side, decreasing the compression damping force will usually increase the feeling of plushness. This is true until you use extremely light compression damping. With very little damping, the plushness can actually decrease. This occurs only on big bumps when the suspension bottoms and therefore feels harsh. On small bumps, less damping still means more plushness.

Let's examine the effects of low-speed compression damping on traction. Imagine you're riding along, and you hit a bump. If there is too little compression damping, the suspension will not have enough resistance as it is being compressed. This means that there is still energy that needs to be dissipated at the crest of the bump, and the wheel will continue to move upward as it crests the bump. This is because the wheel itself has mass. As that mass is moving upward, it wants to remain in motion and continues to move upward, compressing the suspension more than the amount required to handle the bump. This will cause the tire to "unweight" and possibly even lose contact with the ground as it crests the bump, causing a loss of traction.

As compression damping is increased, this phenomenon decreases, and traction improves. If excessive compression damping is used, there will be too much resistance to movement, thereby pushing the center of gravity of the motorcycle, or the sprung mass, upward. Not only can this cause an uncomfortable or harsh ride, but this upward velocity of the chassis tends to unweight the wheel as well, resulting in a loss of traction. In extreme cases, the wheel will come entirely off the ground and skip over the bumps. This is one of the reasons why in bumpy turns at extreme lean angles you may experience difficulty holding an inside cornering line. The bike will tend to drift to the outside of the turn because of this loss of traction.

The last curve on the graph represents maximum dynamic dive, or bottoming resistance. This is distinctly different from static sag, which is measured without the bike moving. Maximum dynamic dive is the amount the suspension compresses when hitting bumps or during braking. The maximum amount of dive is determined by a combination of the spring force and the compression-damping force that resists it. If there is no damping of any kind, the front end will dive and begin to oscillate up and down. If you're braking for a long period of time, friction will eventually stop the oscillation, and you will notice that the fork is compressed, even while still on the brakes. This is called the dynamic ride height. Since damping is nonexistent when there is no suspension movement, the amount the forks are compressed is determined solely by spring forces. However, maximum dynamic dive, or the amount it overshoots the dynamic ride height, is affected by compression damping. Using more compression damping makes the forks compress slower and will tend to hold the chassis up.

If you're hitting a series of bumps with too much compression damping, the suspension will actually extend, growing taller as the wheels hit successive bumps. This is the opposite of the packing discussed earlier.

There are obvious trade-offs between the two extremes of compression-damping settings. As bottoming resistance increases, plushness and maximum dynamic dive both decrease. At some point between these extremes, traction is maximized. Street bikes fare better because they are biased with less compression damping than road race bikes. Remember, you will pay the price for too much or too little compression damping. One of the biggest misconceptions about compression damping is that the faster you ride, the more you need. The right approach is to determine proper spring rates and use only as much compression damping as you need to control suspension bottoming and front-end dive. You can see a chart of proper spring rates for street bikes on page 26. Keep in mind that compression damping is dependent on suspension movement. If there is no movement, there is no damping. Also be aware that the shape of the damping curve is critical, reflecting not only how much damping you have, but how progressive it is.

Now that you have a solid understanding of traction, steering, and suspension basics, it's time to understand how your mind impacts your riding and find out what you can do to maximize its efficiency. Soon you'll be in the perfect mental state to learn advanced techniques faster and more proficiently than you ever thought possible.

Chapter 4
Fear

Fear is the single biggest hindrance we motorcyclists face when trying to improve our skills, yet few riders ever seriously confront it. To make matters worse, it is seldom written about in motorcycle magazines or books, and rarely dealt with in the popular riding schools. If there is one thing that I've learned in the five years I've been conducting my Advanced Riding Clinics, it's that by removing fear, the barriers to learning disappear. After all, anyone can follow step-by-step directions. It's fear that keeps riders from following through on their desires to make a change in their riding.

Dr. Susan Jeffers, author of *Feel the Fear and Do It Anyway*, points out that all fears are fueled by the belief that "I can't handle it." If you're afraid that you can't handle something, like going into that turn 10 miles per hour faster than you usually do, your body's survival mechanisms will make you incapable of pushing through the barrier. Although your conscious mind may want to turn the throttle a little more, your unconscious mind will not allow your wrist to comply. This is a frustrating situation for riders who are serious about improving their skills, but are unaware of what is stopping them from making progress.

Few things strike fear into the hearts of professional racers like the threat of an oily track. Here a giant turbine blows the oil dry off Daytona International Speedway as part of a crash cleanup. Every racer will have to decide how much faith he has in the condition of the track, as well as his tires, when the green flag drops again. Those who have faith, tempered with the knowledge of previous similar experiences, hold a serious advantage.

First, it should be noted that fear is actually a good thing. We must, however, learn to work with it rather than struggle against it, to make it a positive influence on our riding. Obviously, fear is necessary for survival. If we weren't afraid of anything (like falling down), we would soon die by doing stupidly dangerous stuff. For instance, if I tried to run the same lap times as Valentino Rossi, I would eventually crash, since I do not possess the necessary riding knowledge nor the physical strength or reflexes needed to challenge him.

Fear can increase your adrenaline flow, which provides added strength in emergencies. You've undoubtedly heard the story of the elderly woman who lifted a car off her trapped son even though she technically didn't have the strength to do it. But fear can also be your worst enemy if you don't learn to control it. Too much of it can have a crippling effect on even the most experienced riders.

Fear Threshold

Every motorcyclist has what I refer to as a "fear threshold." A fear threshold is a point at which the level of fear becomes so great that the rider's mind cannot process any additional information. This is not unlike trying to run a math-intensive software program on an old computer. It can only make so many calculations per second. If you try throwing too much information at it too quickly, it's liable to crash. In the same way, if you try pushing a motorcycle faster than your brain can disseminate the sensory inputs, you also may crash.

While riding motocross at a friend's practice track many years ago, I came face to face with this reality. In fact, I overshot my fear threshold by such a margin that my mind hit its own reset button so I didn't have to watch what was about to happen.

My buddy Dave was one of those lucky kids whose dad let him build his own motocross track on the family

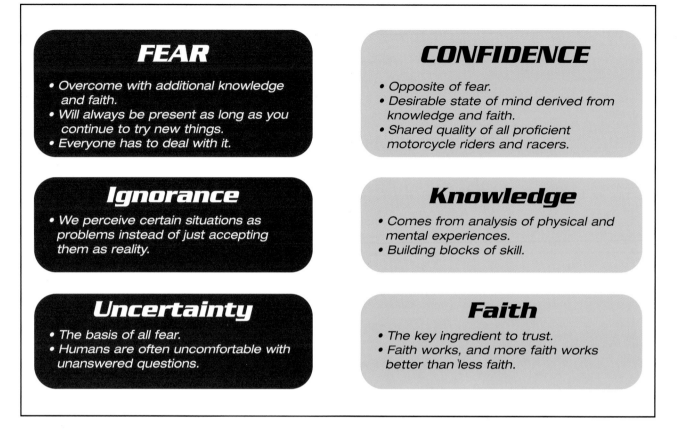

FEAR

- Overcome with additional knowledge and faith.
- Will always be present as long as you continue to try new things.
- Everyone has to deal with it.

Ignorance

- We perceive certain situations as problems instead of just accepting them as reality.

Uncertainty

- The basis of all fear.
- Humans are often uncomfortable with unanswered questions.

CONFIDENCE

- Opposite of fear.
- Desirable state of mind derived from knowledge and faith.
- Shared quality of all proficient motorcycle riders and racers.

Knowledge

- Comes from analysis of physical and mental experiences.
- Building blocks of skill.

Faith

- The key ingredient to trust.
- Faith works, and more faith works better than less faith.

Moving from a state of fear to state of confidence is the single most important factor in being able to learn new skills and avoid accidents. Learning how to be okay with whatever life gives you is the secret.

farm. One day while racing around on my RM80, I came around a turn a little too fast to hit the next jump on my under-sprung bike, so I decided to take a detour around the jump. Unfortunately, I learned too late that my planned escape route had a four-foot-deep ditch in the middle of it.

As it turned out, rather than getting loads of dirt delivered to build the track, Dave got the raw material for the jumps by simply digging it up from the area next to the jump. As soon as I realized what was about to happen, I actually fainted while riding the bike. My mind literally shut down to avoid being conscious for the ensuing carnage. Apparently, it knew the next two seconds were going to be big-time trouble, so it went into "sleep" mode, ostensibly to save me from consciously experiencing the horror.

When I awoke, I was upside down in the ditch with a pretty good headache, and the bike laying on top of me. I had absolutely no recollection of the crash, and, in retrospect, I think that's a good thing.

Often, right before a rider crashes, he says to himself, "I think I'm going to crash." Sure enough, that's exactly what happens. The rule of thumb here is that if you think you will or you think you won't, you're right. In other words, your attitude toward your situation actually makes it real. The reason for this? The power of faith.

The Power of Faith

The opposite of fear is confidence or certainty. Confidence is a state of mind, an attitude based on your knowledge and faith. Knowledge comes from the analysis of physical and mental experiences. Faith is a trust in your knowledge.

Four-time American Motorcyclist Association (AMA) Formula One Champion Mike Baldwin predicted that Wayne Rainey would be a big success even before Rainey left for Europe, a place where he went on to win three world championships. "I could never make myself completely trust the front tire," Baldwin said. "But Wayne had the ability, when the race started, to just decide to trust it, and ride as though it would grip every time." This kind of trust comes from confidence. Put simply, Rainey had total faith that the front tire would stick. And faith is a powerful force in the universe.

The best definition for faith I've ever heard was told to me by my former receptionist. She said that faith was "a force of imagination." If you think about it, this makes perfect sense. Through faith, millions of people from all the world's religions have achieved great things, even though they have such different, and often contrary, beliefs. That's because what you believe in is not as important as the fact that you believe in something. The real creative force is your mind's ability to imagine possibility.

Working with particle accelerators in high-energy physics labs, quantum-mechanics physicists have discovered that it is impossible to observe sub-atomic phenomena without actually *changing* what happens. Amazing as it sounds, you cannot watch something, including yourself and your environment, without creating a new reality. This is why every major sport psychologist emphasizes visualization techniques. By imagining a particular event, you actually create the possibility of its existence.

The stronger your beliefs, the more you affect your environment. A powerful enough belief in tire traction will actually manifest itself with additional grip. This is not the stuff of fairy tales. I have seen it in practice, and it actually helped me win a national road racing championship. Conversely, a terrible fear of losing traction can actually manifest itself in a slideout. This is why all champion racers have such confidence in their abilities. It's not a matter of ego; it's a matter of survival!

How many times have you seen two racers on equal equipment and tires go through a turn at the same speed and yet watched only one of them crash? Sometimes it's a case of one rider making a mistake, but other times it comes down to the difference in confidence level. The more faith you have, the more confident you will be. This is one of the reasons why motorcycling has so often been described as a religious experience.

Although some people would lead you to believe that there is only one true belief system that works, history has clearly demonstrated that anyone with enough faith in their beliefs can be a powerful force. It doesn't matter if you want to attribute your faith, or your results, to something beyond yourself. It all works the same. In other words, there is no such thing as good faith or bad faith, only more faith and less faith. More is better.

No Problem

In the *Tao Te Ching*, Lao Tzu says that "he who is not afraid will always be safe." There are many interpretations of this saying. However, when it comes to motorcycling, I have found one interpretation to have profound significance. It can be explained by inquiring into what happens when your bike begins to slide.

Most motorcyclists have, at one time or another, slid one or both wheels in a corner. This usually occurs under power while exiting a turn, often in the rain. When this happens, what's your reaction? A superior rider will simply let the slide occur as if it were supposed to happen. If you are able to retain your composure, the bike will usually correct itself as if nothing ever happened. That's the purpose of trail in a chassis. It makes the bike want to straighten up whenever it's crooked.

The problem most of us face, however, is that whenever we think that what *is* happening should *not be* happening, we perceive this as a problem and get scared. Once you get scared, your body gets tense and your mind goes into overload. In this situation, you are like a beginning rider and unable to process all the inputs. You have lost your connection with the outer environment and have become focused on your inner fear. At this point, your chances of crashing have increased significantly. Learning to avoid this scenario requires some special practice.

Only by practicing sliding will you become comfortable enough with it that you will not be pushed beyond your fear threshold when it occurs. Because sliding on the street, especially on a large touring bike, can be very dangerous, your best bet is to practice on an off-road or dual-sportbike. The lighter weight of the bike and the slicker surface of the dirt will teach you the dynamics of sliding in a much safer environment. Better still, sign up for a session of American Supercamp (www.american-supercamp.com; 970-674-9434). This is the best place I know to learn the art of sliding.

While riding in the dirt, you will begin to learn that it's okay for your bike to slide and you can just let it happen without fighting it. After all, once you're sliding, there's nothing else for you to do except let it happen. Then when it occurs on the street, you will be able to deal with it without overdosing on fear.

Action Muscle

Another important skill to employ in the war on fear is what Tony Robbins calls "exercising your action muscle." This can be explained as the mental gumption to go into physical action in the face of fear. For example, I have been a singer my entire life, yet I still get serious stage fright almost every time I get up to perform. While racing in a 1994 national road race at Road Atlanta, I was asked to sing the national anthem in front of 24,000 people. Even though I had performed that song hundreds of times in front of much smaller crowds, the large venue had me so nervous my shaking hands could barely hold the microphone still. Although I was almost paralyzed with fear, I was able to close my eyes, take a deep breath, and get up and do it anyway. It was my previous experience that enabled me to do this. It was not my singing practice that prepared me, mind you, but my performing-while-nervous practice.

Over a period of years, I had conditioned myself to view my fear as a signal that it was time to perform. I was actually thankful that it pumped up my adrenaline level because it allowed me to really belt out the tunes. Had I not practiced performing with fear so many times before, I never would have been able to muster the strength to handle all that nervousness. I cannot emphasize enough the importance of practice.

The best way to insure that you will be able to perform in a crisis is to have years of practice under your belt. Whenever you bump up against your fear threshold, your body will do what it has practiced doing. In other words, in times of trouble, you go with what you know. If you interpret fear as a signal to increase your alertness, you will be able to use it to your advantage. When learning new skills, it's best to always push yourself just enough to feel a little fear and get in the habit of riding within it. That way, when the unexpected takes you by surprise, you'll be able to handle the feeling without shutting down.

Bravery

Brave people aren't simply those who can overcome larger amounts of fear. Instead, brave people are the ones who raise the level of the point at which fear gets control of their minds. For example, Mick Doohan couldn't ride any faster than you if he experienced the same fears you do while riding your pace. The difference in his ability simply means that the speeds at which he experiences those fears are much higher than yours.

Once he reaches that threshold, he can't break through it anymore than we can break through ours. It's his way of thinking that makes the difference.

As soon as your mind reaches this "information overload" point, you'll need to re-center yourself as quickly as possible. Hopefully, you'll be able to accomplish this before you get out of control. To do this, you need to know how to concentrate.

In an emergency your body is programmed to "go with what you know." If you've not practiced riding with a little bit of fear, you will likely panic when subjected to an unexpected event.

Chapter 5
Concentration

In the quest for maximum bike control, your mental ability to be completely present in the moment is just as important as your actual riding skills. Because the penalties for not paying attention while riding are so severe, the act of motorcycling all but forces you to pay close attention. For this reason, motorcycling has been called "the lazy man's Zen," as it can produce the same type of spiritual awareness as deep meditation. Fear and distraction are the enemies of presence, and concentration is the cure.

Have you ever noticed how difficult it is to talk to someone in a crowded room? With many people talking at once, it's difficult to concentrate on what you're saying. Similarly, when riding motorcycles, there are many distractions that hinder concentration on the road. A motorcyclist's ability to concentrate is probably his most important tool for staying alive, yet few riders have any training in how to do it effectively. We often use the word, but just what do we mean when we talk about concentration?

Three-time National Karate Champion and motorcycle racer Ken Marena defines proper concentration as "relaxed attentiveness." In other words,

Even a moment's lapse of concentration can have disastrous results. Understanding and practicing concentration techniques is just as important as your physical skills in being safe.

concentration means being aware of your surroundings without stressing out your body. Because all of us eventually fatigue from any prolonged activity, Marena stresses the importance of getting proper rest before and after long periods of intense concentration for optimum performance.

According to Webster's dictionary, concentration is "the act of bringing or directing toward a common center or objective: focus." Using this definition as a starting point, let's take a look at how concentration works and discuss how you can improve your degree of proficiency.

How It Works

In order to master something, you must first identify what it is. Often this is accomplished by starting with what it is not. One by one, you discount the possibilities until you end up with an idea of what you're facing. At this point, you can decide where you want to go, and you can focus your attention toward it. This is not unlike eliminating each of the voices in a crowded room until you're able to carry on a conversation with just one person.

L. Ron Hubbard calls a person who is a master of concentration a "clear," someone who's clear of his own mind's distractions. Although everyone's mind

wanders from time to time, the ability to re-center oneself varies greatly from person to person. A master is simply someone who's highly skilled at this process.

In his book *The Use and Abuse of History,* Friedrich Nietzsche emphasizes the value of living "unhistorically." This is the act of being fully present in the moment by temporarily forgetting past events that get in the way of our concentration. He says that the man of action "forgets most things in order to do one. He is unjust to what is behind him, and only recognizes one law— the law of that which is to be."

Neuroscientists believe that the human brain can focus its attention on up to seven things at once before it loses the ability to concentrate. Keith Code, in his groundbreaking book *The Twist of the Wrist*, describes this process in terms of spending money. Code writes: "Attention, and where you spend it while riding a motorcycle, is a key element in how well you will function. Attention has its limits. Each person has a certain amount of it, and the amount varies from individual to individual. You have a fixed amount of attention just as you have a fixed amount of money. Let's say you have a $10 bill's worth of attention. If you spend $5 of it on one aspect of riding, you have only $5 left for all the other aspects. Spend $9 and you only have $1 left, and so on." Because reality comes at you from all sides, you must constantly be choosing which things to pay attention to and which ones to ignore. You can do this by tuning in the requisite and tuning out the extraneous. Experience is what helps you decide what things are to be paid attention to as well as which ones should be ignored. This is why beginners shouldn't try the skills in this book. It's too risky for them to practice advanced techniques because they don't have enough experience to recognize the warning signs of a bike that is about to crash.

When it comes right down to it, concentration is the elimination of outside, or inside, distractions. When there's nothing to distract you, you are fully present in the moment. In Zen, this is called *mu shin*, literally "no mind." At this point, all things are possible. For motorcyclists, this is the ability to react to circumstances without hesitation. Racers call it being "in the zone."

Being In the Zone

Before you can get in the zone in any activity, you first must practice your techniques over and over. The skills must become second nature, and you shouldn't have to think about them. Your actions will seemingly happen automatically, and you can react instantaneously to any situation. Just as you don't have to think how to breathe or how to beat your own heart or even walk, when riding in the zone, the correct inputs will happen as a matter of natural course. In this state, all your awareness is spent on what to react to, not how to react.

Awareness is the process of information integration; it's your ability to discern the key elements of information on the fly based on a much larger pool of incoming data. Any given riding situation requires a specific amount of awareness to properly negotiate. Once you hone your skills to a high level, you will notice that it takes less and less attention to accomplish a specific goal. Of course, this can become a dangerous situation. It is tempting to only use the minimum amount of awareness necessary for a given situation so you can use your "excess processing power" on other activities. For instance, you may think about what you want to eat at your next stop while riding your motorcycle. I am a firm believer in awareness overkill. In other words, keep all of your attention on what you're doing right now. This gives you a reserve of "what if" ability to deal with unexpected occurrences such as another vehicle coming into your lane.

You can tell that you're in the zone because you won't have to block thoughts from your mind. Werner Erhard wrote, "What you resist persists." If you stop resisting things like fear and uncertainty, and just allow them to pass through you, they will disappear, and your actions will become pure.

In actual practice, you don't know you're in the zone while you're there. The moment that you consciously contemplate your performance, you have left it. You only recognize it when you leave it, by comparing it to the previous moment's lack of conscious reflection. This is different from when we are sleeping, because we don't have awareness of our environment while we sleep. When we're in the zone, we have total awareness of our environment, but don't make internal commentary about it.

Improving Concentration

Practice is the secret to improving concentration. But this is a different kind of practice than most people are used to because it involves the doing of a non-action. This practice is best described by a Chinese man reported to be oldest living person on Earth. When asked what the secret to his longevity was, he responded, "Inner quiet." Because the single biggest distraction you face is the constant interruptions from your own mind, the practice of inner quiet is crucial for superior concentration. The result is increased awareness and, ultimately, better control.

To achieve inner quiet, what Buddhists call "the still mind," means to stop consciously thinking about things. But a still mind is not a stupid mind. Rather, it is a mind ready for whatever presents itself. This is not "zoning-out" like we all tend to do from time to time; it is "zoning *in*." When you have no thoughts to distract you, the full use of all your skills and abilities becomes available.

Many factors can prevent you from achieving inner quiet. As we learned in the last chapter, fear and uncertainty are two of them. Furthermore, you need to be able to control your mind to prevent it from wandering. To learn how to do anything, it is necessary to begin with the basics. Remember how difficult operating a clutch was when you first began? Now you can do it without thinking about it. Achieving inner quiet is a similar process.

Meditation Practice

Meditation is probably the best way to practice inner quiet and reduce stress. There isn't enough space here to provide a complete explanation of meditation techniques, but there's one exercise anyone can do that I find to be particularly helpful.

You can practice achieving inner quiet alone in a room, walking, lying down, and even out on the road. Simply try to think of nothing. At some point, you will find yourself thinking something. As soon as you notice the thought, put it out of your mind so you are left with no internal communication. This is much more difficult than it sounds. You'll be amazed by how much "noise" there is inside your head. Your brain can be bombarded with everything from "Check out that blonde" to "Don't forget to pick up peanut butter."

Constant thoughts are not unlike the sounds in that crowded room of people. It's no wonder we get confused and afraid; there's a party going on up there. One by one, just ask the guests to leave. If you work at it, you can eventually get them all to leave. The process

The mind can only handle up to seven issues at one time. Being able to discern what's important from what isn't is critical in high-performance situations. In the corkscrew at Laguna Seca, riders must deal with directional, speed, and elevation changes, while simultaneously monitoring their bikes' systems and the other riders' actions. It is as much a mental workout as a physical one.

Retrospective analysis of your experience will help for the next ride. Talk about what worked and what didn't work with a riding buddy. Remember, the act of speaking makes concepts much more real than just thinking about them.

can be very therapeutic, especially while riding. By practicing this, your mind will become more still, and your concentration will improve.

Warning Signs

Concentration can be affected by many physical conditions. Low blood sugar, not enough rest, and controlled substances all have detrimental effects on your ability to concentrate. It's also important to do a self-diagnostic test every once in awhile to make sure your stress level isn't getting out of control. The symptoms are easy to spot as mental stress quickly manifests itself in your body. In Western culture, we brace ourselves for that proverbial gut punch by tightening up our stomachs, shoulders, arms, and hands. Not only does that unnecessarily fatigue our muscles, but it prevents proper breathing.

Deep, relaxed breaths help bring oxygen to the body. This allows muscles to operate freely and at peak efficiency, which enables you to concentrate on your environment, and not be distracted by your stress. Proper breathing utilizes a "belly breath" not a "chest breath." Babies do this naturally, but over time they become socialized to hold in stress by taking shorter, more forced breaths. By putting your hand on your belly, you should feel air going in and out without any muscle tension. If your chest is doing most of the moving, it's time to focus your attention on your breathing until it becomes easy and natural again. Remember, true concentration is trying not to concentrate.

Chapter 6
Right Attitude

Before trying out any new riding skills, it's important to make sure you are in a mental state that is conducive to learning. If you're like most hard-core motorcycle enthusiasts, no matter how many riding skills, books or magazine articles you read and no matter how hard you practice, you will get frustrated with your progress at some point. The secret to ending this frustration is having the right attitude.

Beginner's Mind

The most critical component of having the right attitude is maintaining what, in Japan, is called *shoshin*, which means "beginner's mind." This is the attitude of a child during his formative years when the majority of learning in the human brain takes place. Zen Master Shunryu Suzuki says, "In the beginner's mind, there are many possibilities; in the expert's mind, there are few."

Not surprisingly, the hallmark of the beginner's mind is humility. Being humble is the key to learning because it is the ego that keeps our minds closed to new ideas. The more you think you know about riding, the less you will be open to new techniques. Therefore, the best policy for learning new things is to always keep a beginner's mind.

A beginner's mind can also be described as living in possibility, as opposed to expectation. Reality has a way of shaping itself to your pre-conceived expectations, so don't give it the opportunity to limit your learning by deciding you already know how to do something. My favorite example of living in possibility is demonstrated by the television character McGuyver. The reason his character is so compelling is because he refuses to let what he already knows get in the way of seeing new possibilities. Rather than accepting popular belief, he looks at everything with the wonder of a child. I'm not suggesting that you figure out how to make your motorcycle into a bomb. I am inviting you to look at your riding from a fresh new perspective, uncluttered from past ideas about how things need to be done.

It's clear from watching the top racers' vast differences in riding styles that there are many approaches that can be effective. Sometimes a racer will even need to change his style from one track to the next. The racers who can keep a beginner's mind and adapt their style to current conditions are the ones who are the most successful. The danger, however, is that the more you apply this practice, the more your mind will tend to anticipate what will happen next. This will make it easier for you to either get bored or compensate for the boredom by pushing too hard. In

Riding while angry or frustrated is never a good idea since you can't concentrate on the road. If you find yourself in this condition, get an attitude adjustment by taking five and clearing your mind of your problems.

finding a comfortable learning pace, you will enjoy your relationship with the road and keep motivated.

Motivation

The second component of right attitude is motivation. You need to be motivated to try something new. For example, if you're in a bad mood, it is difficult to learn new skills as your mind is preoccupied with unrelated thoughts that keep it from being clear. The clearer your mind is, the easier it is to understand new information. And the easier it is, the faster you will learn. If you work on your skills alone, it is easy to become frustrated, but the frustration itself is encouraging. It is your mind's way of signaling that you have lost the right attitude, and that it is time to re-center yourself.

Practicing with a riding buddy is one of the best ways I know to keep motivated. Not only can he see

Visualization is an important technique in developing a positive road relationship. By imagining that you and the bike are one, you can go with the flow of the road much like a good phonograph needle effortlessly follows every nuance of a record.

Riding your bike when your mind's not right is a good way to get arrested or worse.

what you are doing and provide valuable feedback, but he can also encourage you when you start to get tired or lazy. This is critical if you are to remain focused on the task at hand. If your mind starts wandering, not only are you not learning, but you are also increasing the likelihood of making a costly mistake that could lead to an accident.

Road Relationship

The third component of right attitude is your "road relationship." As motorcyclists, we like to spend a lot of time on the open road, but few of us ever really consider our relationship to it. Whether you ride fast or slow, you have an unwritten agreement with the road beneath you.

Like family or business relationships, your road relationship can take three basic forms: indifferent,

adversarial, or complementary. An indifferent relationship is like the one you have with the cashier at a fast-food joint. You neither like nor dislike the cashier—you just deal with the person to reach the objective, which is ordering a hamburger or paying for french fries. Most riders have an indifferent road relationship. They think of it a little as possible and don't really relate to the road except when there is a perceived danger, in which case they approach it with caution and distrust. This is a normal survival response, but it can also get you into trouble if you don't learn to manage it.

Another popular road relationship is of the adversarial variety. This is usually seen in sport and dual-sport riders. It is fueled by the notion that they're going to beat the road into submission. The road becomes their enemy, and they set out to do battle with it. A famous riding instructor advises: "You don't beat your competitors. You beat the track better than they did." The problem with this attitude is that, just as it is difficult to communicate with someone who disagrees with you, it is difficult to be sensitive to small changes in pavement when you don't like the road.

The most beneficial type of road relationship is a complementary one. In this kind of relationship, you work *with* the road instead of *against* it. Dealing with your fear and maximizing your concentration are both skills needed to achieve the right attitude. They are necessary to learn skills and improve your riding. Unfortunately, many skilled riders lack a positive road relationship. Although you don't get to pick your family members, you do get to decide what kind of relationship you're going to have with them. Similarly, you get to decide what kind of relationship you're going to have with the road.

Legendary motocross champion Bob Hannah is a great example of someone who knows how to relate to the road. Hannah used to like to race in the rain. This is not because he particularly enjoyed getting dirty, but because he knew that everyone else hated it. He realized that if he could approach it with the right attitude, he'd have a big advantage over his competition. With several national championships under his belt, it's difficult to argue with his logic.

So, how do you create a positive road relationship? Perhaps the best way is by using visualization techniques to get you in the right state of mind. Before I ride, I like to think about positive past experiences, times when I had a great ride and everything just seemed to click. I close my eyes and remember what the road and scenery looked like, how the air smelled, and what sounds I heard. I completely immerse myself in the memory until I feel like I'm actually there. There are physiological changes that take place during this inner journey that put my mind at ease, and my body automatically relaxes.

Once I have conjured up the memory in my mind, I say some of my favorite affirmations aloud. I speak, not just think, phrases like "the bike and I are one," and "the cosmic rhythm flows through me." I realize this sounds corny, but it's an incredibly effective process for re-centering yourself in the here and now, which naturally gives you a positive road relationship. For example, when I say, "The bike and I are one," I imagine such a close connection to the bike that I don't know where it ends and I begin.

A positive road relationship also includes knowing how to deal with traffic. In Southern California, where motorcycles can legally ride between the cars in slow traffic, it is imperative that motorcyclists have the right attitude. When I moved to California in 1992, I remember being terrified of this "lane splitting." I thought of cars as enemies and had several close calls that left me feeling pretty scared. But, in time, I began to change my attitude toward the traffic, and I started thinking of it as more of a dodging game. Now I rarely have close calls, and when I do, I don't freak out and panic. I just simply do whatever's necessary to avoid an accident. This makes me a much safer rider, since a moment's lapse of concentration anywhere can be fatal.

Enjoyment

The last factor in creating the right attitude is the ability to enjoy what you are doing. You have to enjoy the process of practicing riding skills. For those of you, who, like me, possess the competitive spirit, you can bring it into your training. Just remember not to take competition too seriously, or you will eventually lose your motivation toward practice. It's fine to compete with other riders or even the stopwatch, but do it in the spirit of a game. For example, if I told you to run 10 feet forward, stop, run 15 feet to the left, 12 feet to the right, then 18 feet back again, you would think it was a boring exercise. But if I put a tennis racquet in your hand and was hitting balls at you, the same activity would be a lot of fun. That's the power of gaming. Think of ways you can make motorcycling into a game by creating exercises that utilize speed, time, and position goals.

If you're learning with a buddy, don't let yourself get so caught up in competing with him that you forget why you are there. Because people learn at different paces, it's important to not push people faster than they can learn. Discuss your goals beforehand and make sure you are both clear about what you are doing as well as why you are doing it.

The best attitude for learning riding—or life—skills I ever heard came from Herb Cohen, author of *You Can Negotiate Anything*. He said, "I care, but not *that* much." In other words, care enough about your practice to put out your best effort, but don't care so much that if you don't make your desired progress, it will bother you.

When you have the right attitude, you become naturally easy-going, and you're able to enjoy your successes and failures as one and the same. Either way, you are learning something new. Both success and failure are important for keeping your attitude from becoming overconfident and reckless, or under-confident and hesitant.

Chapter 7
Vision

The majority of decisions made while riding are based on information coming in through your eyes. In basic terms, your eyes should be up to snuff, displaying 20/20 vision or better. But *how* you use your eyes is just as important as having properly functioning ones. Using your eyes skillfully requires some understanding of how you react to what you see.

Spotlight vs. Floodlight

What you are able to see is based not only on the amount of light available, but also on the types of things upon which you choose to concentrate. Some people choose to illuminate the world with a spotlight. Others view their surroundings with a floodlight. A spotlight highlights a small area in great detail whereas a floodlight illuminates a larger area with less intensity.

In the American education system, much emphasis is placed on discovering life's details. We use microscopes and telescopes to examine things both near and far. We use computers to analyze the world by breaking it up into micro-sized bits. We have, in essence, been trained to rely on the spotlight and forget about the floodlight.

Growing up, the only floodlight-type training I received was in driver's education class. Some of you might remember the Smith Driving System developed in the 1950s. In that system, one of the tenets of good driving was to "get the big picture." Actually, Smith was right on the money. Using your vision as a floodlight slows down your "sense of speed" and allows you to be aware of more potential hazards and opportunities.

Sense of Speed

It's important to make a distinction between your actual speed and your perceived sense of speed. Your mind can play tricks on you when you rely on your spotlight vision while operating a moving vehicle. For instance, if you look at the ground directly beneath you while riding, it seems like you're moving at a million miles per hour. If you then change your focus and look at the mountains in the background, it feels like you're barely moving at all even though your actual speed hasn't changed.

Keith Code once told me of an experiment he performed to examine the perception of speed. He took a piece of paper and cut two "eye holes" in it and then tried to drive his car by looking through the small openings. He said that even driving straight down an empty road was terrifying when forced to see through the little holes because the sense of speed was tremendously increased.

Even professional racers don't always look through the corner, and they're just as susceptible to getting tense as everyone else when they can't see where they're going. Notice how Miguel Duhamel (#17) is looking through the turn and his outside arm is completely relaxed. Kurtis Roberts (#80), while in the same turn at Daytona, is looking straight ahead and his outside arm is so tense his elbow is pointing in the air, motocross style.

When you're riding over your head, you develop a similar sense that things are moving too fast. This is called target fixation, and occurs when you narrow your perspective to the spotlight view. As a result, you will have the sense that things are moving too fast. The solution to target fixation is to widen your perspective to the floodlight view because the bigger the viewing area, the slower things seem to move. Widening your viewing area certainly takes practice, but the farther ahead you look in a turn, the better off you will be.

Looking through Turns

There are three important reasons for looking as far through a turn as possible. For starters, the farther ahead you look, the earlier you will recognize any potential hazards and the sooner you'll be able to spot opportunities for early acceleration. The second reason is to slow down your sense of speed, which will go a long way toward reducing any anxiety you may have about a turn. This will allow your body to stay relaxed and permit your mind to see the big picture. The third

Before entering any corner it's critical that you look as far through it as you can. This slows down your "sense of speed" and prepares you for what's up ahead.

reason to look far through turns is that your body naturally wants to go in the direction it is looking. That's why when riders target fixate, they often run right into whatever it was they were looking at. In other words, where you look is where you go.

Of course, before you look through the turn, you first must decide where your turning point will be. This requires a quick burst of spotlight vision, followed by a switch to the floodlight view through the corner. Code likes to call this visual quick-change the "two-step."

The best practice for looking through turns is to set up a circle in a clean parking lot and have a buddy stand in the center of it. You should be able to look at, or even through, him for an entire revolution. He will be able to tell if you panic and look forward because he will be watching your eyes. This is much more difficult than it sounds but can be learned fairly quickly. I recommend doing this at a very slow speed until you are comfortable with the drill. There is no need to go fast as the important thing here is to train your head to be turned enough to see the center of the circle.

Take your time practicing this drill until you can do it effortlessly. The ability is a perquisite for every cornering skill in this book, so make sure you have it down before trying anything else. The good news is that once you have mastered looking through the turn, everything else will seem a lot easier.

Chapter 8
Line Selection

There is no perfect "line" or path of travel for every corner. Speed, road conditions, hazards, and rider skill all play a role in choosing which line to take in a particular turn. After training hundreds of students, both street riders and racers, I discovered that there are three primary "line" related mistakes made when cornering. All can easily be corrected with a little knowledge and some self-evaluation.

The first cornering problem is turning too soon. Not turning quickly enough at the entrance is the second problem. And the last problem is making numerous mid-turn corrections as you ride through the corner. I'll discuss each of these common mistakes, errors made by both experienced and novice riders. I'll also describe some effective lines to take given perfect conditions and will point out important line exceptions when alternative tactics must be employed.

Premature Initiation

Many riders grow anxious as they approach a turn. They worry about their corner entry speed, how hard to brake, and if their tires will have enough traction to see them through the turn. With all this going on, inside their heads, and the corner getting closer and closer, it becomes difficult for them to wait for the appropriate time to begin the turn, and they end up initiating it prematurely (figure 1).

As discussed in the last chapter, it's important to look through the turn before you enter it. This makes it even more difficult to wait for the appropriate time because your body naturally wants to go where your eyes are looking. It takes some practice to train yourself to keep going straight while you're looking somewhere else, but it pays big dividends by the time you're ready to exit the corner.

The good news is that by looking far through the corner, your perception of speed slows way down. This goes a long way toward reducing the anxiety you feel when approaching the turn. It also helps you relax and follow your intended line through the corner. If you look at the big picture instead of concentrating on one small area, you'll be better able to see the entire turn and be able to consider all the possibilities for getting through it safely.

Initiating too soon often happens when the rider fixates on the inside of the turn. As this "fixed" target gets closer, it is often incorrectly used as a reference point for initiating the turn. One consequence of taking a turn too early is that you will be committed to a line that takes you to the outside of the exit and leaves you little opportunity to change course mid-corner should the need arise. Turning in early forces you to the outside of the turn at the exit because you run out of room on the inside to get enough lean angle to make the turn. This means you will need to do a lot of turning after the apex of the turn, which commits you to full lean for the remainder of the turn all the way until your exit point.

Additionally, if you are at the point of maximum lean angle and a mid-corner correction is required, you may run out of ground clearance and start scraping hard parts. This is especially serious on bikes with limited clearance, like cruisers or any bike coming in at a high rate of speed.

Although a late turn-in certainly helps racers go faster around tracks, the technique is even more important in street riding. By covering more real estate before starting the actual turn, you get a better view around the corner *before* you decide on, and commit to, a line. As seen in figure 1, your line of sight will offer a better angle to reveal things (especially in blind corners) like oncoming vehicles, things that might otherwise be discovered too late if evasive maneuvers are in order. As a general rule of thumb, it is always better to err on the side of a slow entry and faster exit than vice versa.

Too high an entry speed usually causes a lot of mistakes to happen in rapid succession and can easily set off a series of events that can lead to a crash. Slowing your entry speed and going deeper into the turn will provide you with a better view of what is coming. Being able to see farther into the turn will allow you to initiate the right lean angle for the arc that you wish to carve through the entire corner and eliminate the need for any mid-turn corrections. If the corner has an increasing radius, you can get on the gas sooner and harder. If the corner has a decreasing radius, like the one shown in figure 4, you still have time to adjust your plan for going through it.

Slow Steering

Slowly initiating a turn (figure 2) when you are traveling at speed can have the same consequences as turning too soon. You risk going off the edge of the road at the exit without a second risky steering input. Quick steering feels very awkward until you have lots of practice doing it. Many riders fear that their motorcycles will slide out from under them if "pitched" over with too much force into a corner. But, with the exception of slippery conditions like rain or gravel, it is extremely rare for someone to crash a bike by simply steering too quickly into a turn. This is even true of most cruisers, whose lack of ground clearance is the limiting factor in cornering speed.

Turning quickly will also allow you to get back on the throttle sooner, which will help stabilize the chassis during cornering. By looking through the turn and quickly steering at the correct point on the road, you not only get the hard work out of the way sooner, but you also buy yourself time to change your intended line based on conditions.

Fifty Pencing

"Fifty pencing" is the term British motorcyclists use for making too many mid-corner directional changes (figure 3). This is because the polygonal shape of a fifty-pence coin, with its multiple flat edges, resembles the path some riders take while traveling through a turn.

Fifty pencing is a very telling sign of a beginning rider at work. A beginner doesn't have enough experience to know how far the bike needs to be turned in order to complete a corner, so he keeps making corrections as he realizes his initial input was insufficient. A new rider often forgets to look through the turn to see where he needs to finish. By only looking where he is going to be in the next second, he will tend to steer toward that imaginary point in the corner. When he looks up, he'll realize that he still needs to turn more to get through the corner. Therefore, he'll initiate another correction, but again will only look at the next immediate point in the turn. He'll find himself in the middle of an inaccurate and inefficient process.

Generally, beginners are not comfortable enough to exert the necessary turning amount all at once. Of course, plenty of experienced riders share some of these same problems to a lesser degree.

If you are having fifty-pencing problems, keep your head up. There's no need to look at the ground—it will

Line Selection

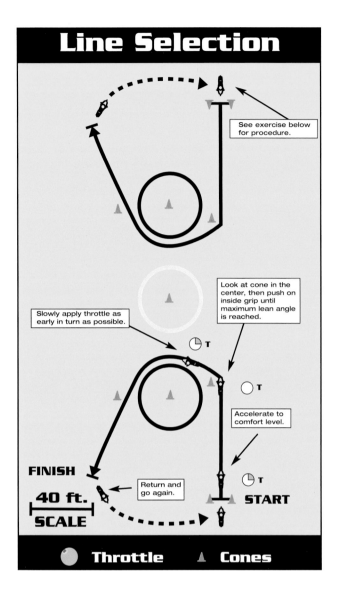

See exercise below for procedure.

Look at cone in the center, then push on inside grip until maximum lean angle is reached.

Slowly apply throttle as early in turn as possible.

Accelerate to comfort level.

FINISH

Return and go again.

40 ft. SCALE

START

● **Throttle**   ▲ **Cones**

the faster you can travel. An arc, by definition, is still a turn. However, by eliminating the three bad habits that I mentioned earlier, you can widen your arc through any turn, thereby allowing yourself more speed or a greater margin of safety.

By delaying your entry point and countersteering quickly to get the bike to maximum lean as rapidly as possible, you will effectively "straighten" the turn as seen in the illustrations. Every time you make a steering input, you add some degree of risk. As a result, it's best to minimize the total number of inputs in any given turn. As you travel through the turn, applying throttle will stabilize the suspension. As the turn opens up you can add throttle as you countersteer out of it to help to straighten the bike up and increase your exit speed. Another consequence of using a quick initial turn-in is that the length of time you must lean over will be minimized. Because every turn requires a specific amount of steering to complete, the longer it takes to do the requisite amount of steering, the more time you will spend leaning over. The more lean angle you have, the less stable the bike becomes and the worse it handles. Getting off the gas or braking while at a high lean angle will cause the bike to straighten up and run wide in the turn. These actions, combined with too much speed, are the precursors of a crash.

Think of the distance you cover while you are leaning over as the "danger zone." The longer you are committed to maximum lean, the longer you are at risk and the less prepared you will be to handle any unexpected complications like road hazards or someone moving into your lane.

Creating the ideal line through a turn starts with the choice of a turning point. This is the position or placement on the road where you initiate the turn by countersteering. Choosing a turning point every time you approach a turn is better than waiting for one to be forced on you either by too much speed or by not being able to see far enough into a corner. By planning ahead, you stay in control of the bike.

Because of the repetitive nature of a racetrack, turns are somewhat easier to predict. However, when navigating a curving mountain road, your turning points will be less exact than those on the track. This doesn't mean that they should be vague. Rather, they should be specifically selected for the road conditions, your speed, and the perceived arc of the approaching turn.

Locating good turning points is a skill that requires some trial-and-error and practice at slower speeds. Heading up an unfamiliar canyon road is not the best

still be there after you complete the turn! Instead, look as far into the turn as possible. When doing so, all the imaginary turning points in your head will vanish. Upon seeing the big picture, it will be much easier to plan and follow a single arc through the corner. As an added bonus, you'll be able to see what's in store up ahead so you'll be prepared.

Arc = Speed

There isn't a perfect line that works best for everyone in a given turn, but there is an "ideal" to think about when choosing your line. One of the most important things to commit to memory is the equation "Arc equals speed." The arc, or radius of a specific turning line, is directly proportional to the amount of speed you can carry through it. In other words, the greater the arc, time to start experimenting with different kinds of turning points. Selecting a turning point will also teach you to avoid slow steering inputs that use up valuable real estate within a corner. Even if your decision ends up being less than ideal, choosing a turning point is always a better plan than not choosing one.

Real World Lines

Ideal lines are most commonly found on a racetrack. On the street, reality rules, and it offers up a variety of distractions and hazards that motorcyclists have to confront. Even roads that you are familiar with are subject to constant and unexpected change. You must be prepared for coming around a blind turn only to find loose gravel, a newly developed pothole, a car partially blocking your lane, or anything else that forces you to have to rethink your chosen line.

In street riding, it's always best to expect the unexpected. To keep from ending up in the hospital, or worse, you must have some line options in reserve.

FIGURE 1: PREMATURE INITIATION

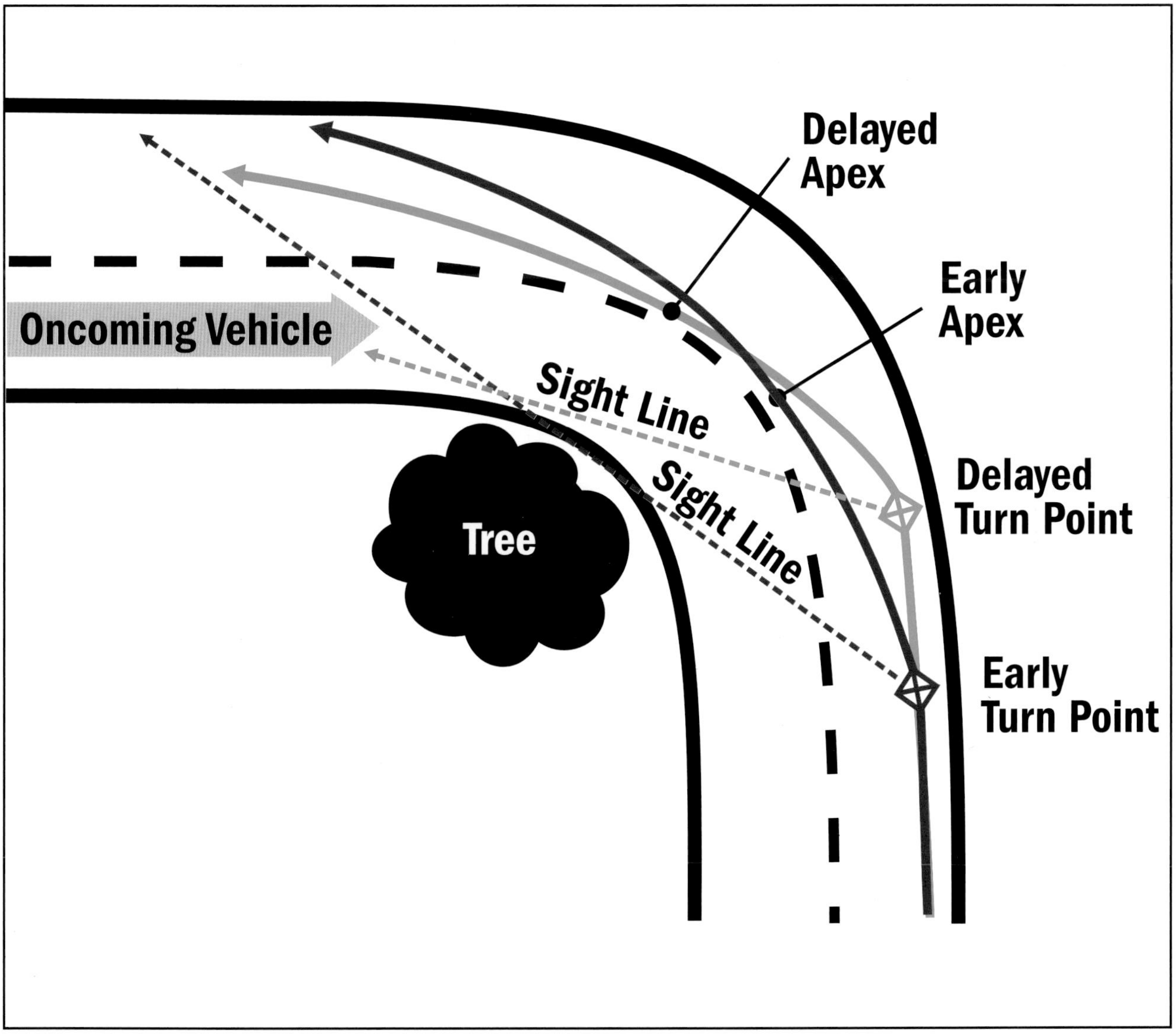

Delayed Apex

Early Apex

Oncoming Vehicle

Sight Line

Sight Line

Tree

Delayed Turn Point

Early Turn Point

The most common line selection mistake is turning too early. Not only does it restrict your ability to see around blind corners, but it forces you to run wide at the exit and limits what mid-corner corrections you can make.

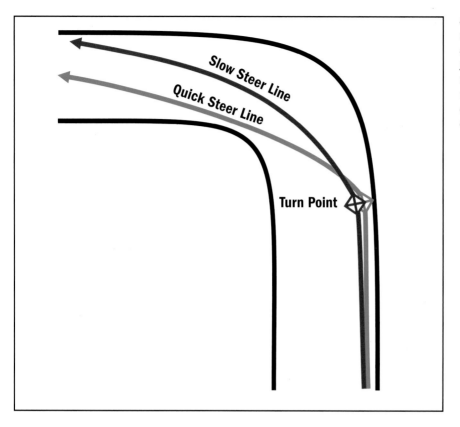

Similar in its consequences to a premature initiation, slow steering into a corner causes you to stay at maximum lean for an extended period of time. A quick steering input can get most of the turning done early in the corner.

FIGURE 3: FIFTY PENCING

Having multiple mid-corner steering corrections is the mark of a beginning rider or a badly misjudged corner. This phenomenon is called "fifty pencing" by British riders due to the line's similarity to the multi-faceted shape of an English fifty pence coin.

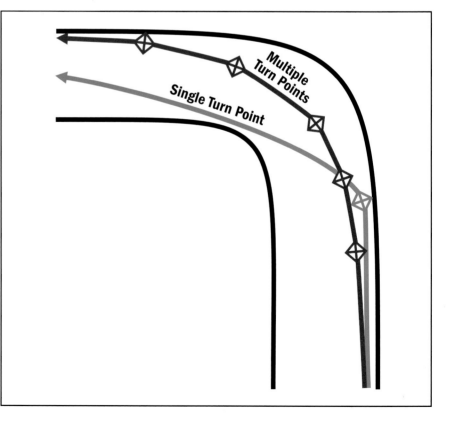

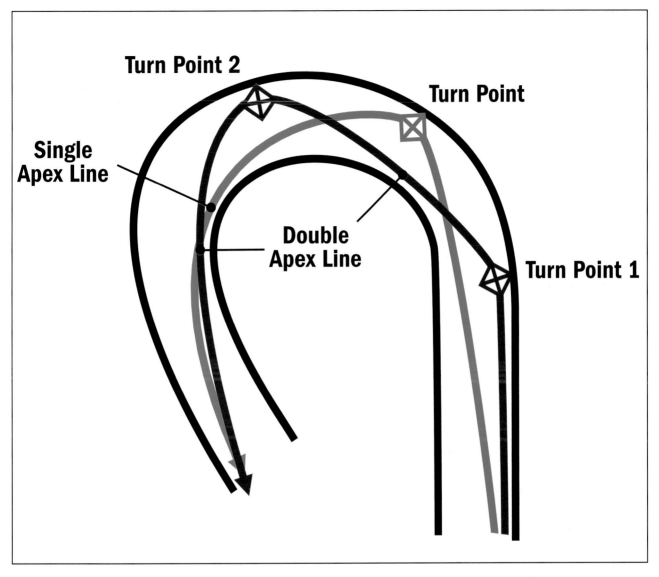

Turn Point 2

Turn Point

Single Apex Line

Double Apex Line

Turn Point 1

The dreaded decreasing radius turn can bite even an experienced rider if he didn't leave plenty of lean angle in reserve. With a delayed entry, it can be safely completed with one turning point.

Keith Code termed this the "Lean Angle Credit Card." If you have too much entry speed, you're committed to your maximum lean angle and hard parts are dragging on the road, your lean angle credit line is going to be over its limit. If any hazard pops up just out of your line of sight, you're going to be overdrawn. To keep from going deeper in debt, so to speak, you need to have some credit left.

Using a slower corner entry speed will allow you to make a mid-corner steering correction to the outside of the turn. This will also leave some lean angle in

reserve so you can make steering adjustments to the inside of the corner. Committing to maximum lean angle and using high entry speeds to get you through a turn in the fastest possible time are practices best left for the track.

Other Types of Turns

In the real world, there are many tricky turns that require a deeper understanding of riding procedure if you want to effectively negotiate them. One of the most difficult types is a decreasing radius turn (figure 4). When

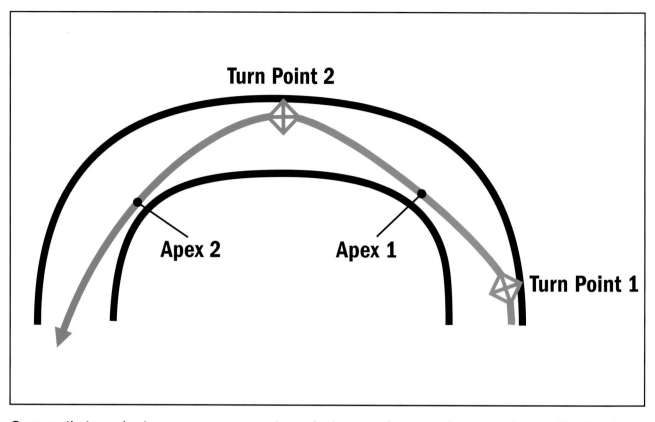

Corners that require two or more apexes to navigate come in many shapes and sizes. The key is to plan as far ahead as possible in picking your turning points, before necessity forces them on you when you least expect it.

entering a blind turn on the street, there is always the possibility that the turn will tighten up. Two riding practices will help in negotiating this type of turn: using slower entry speeds and choosing deeper turning points.

As a rule of thumb, if you are traveling through a turn and the inside and outside lines of the road appear to be coming together, this means that the radius is decreasing. If the inside and outside lines start to separate, the turn is starting to straighten out. This signifies that the radius is increasing, and you will be able to open the throttle earlier and harder.

Another non-standard type of turn is one that requires a double apex (figure 5). A double apex turn, by definition, will require at least one mid-turn correction. You can readjust your line of travel by increasing pressure on the inside handlebar or by initiating a slight rolling off of the throttle. If you have to use a lot of brakes, it is probably a result of either too much entry speed or a blind turn where you did not leave enough reserve lean angle for the unexpected.

Practicing Lines

You can always learn something about the best line through a turn by just riding through it. But speeding up your learning curve will only happen if you take a more deliberate approach. The safest and cheapest method is to set up cones in a vacant parking lot that has good traction. By trying several different turn points and lines through your practice turn, you will quickly see what works best for your type of motorcycle and riding style. Use cones to mark brake on and off points and to indicate where to get back on the throttle. Practicing the same turn at different speeds will help you find your weaknesses and give you specific skills to address.

Start with a turn that has a constant radius and practice using only one steering input. After you feel comfortable with the "standard" turn, set one up with a decreasing radius or double apex. Start at slower speeds and experiment using several turn points until

Choosing a proper line requires mental preparation and a good view of where you're about to turn.

you feel comfortable. Try increasing your corner entry speeds gradually using the same turn points but adding a quicker steering input to compensate for the higher speed. These skills can be easily transferred to the street, and, if you can find an interesting turn without too much traffic, try placing cones on the side of the road to mark reference points for turning and braking. Having one or more of your riding buddies along will help you with feedback as others can often see what you are doing wrong and will be able to offer suggestions.

Chapter 9
Throttle Control

The single most important control on your motor-cycle is the throttle. This is because it applies forces to so many aspects of your bike's handling including: traction, suspension, weight transfer, steering, stability, ground clearance, and of course, speed. Knowing how to skillfully apply the throttle is one of the major distinctions between good riders and great riders.

Throttle Effects

To understand proper throttle usage, you first need to be aware of what happens to the bike when the throttle is applied in either direction. In a straight line, the throttle obviously causes the engine speed to increase, propelling the bike forward. As this goes on, other happenings also take place.

Because motorcycle tires have variable profiles, your effective gearing changes depending on lean angle. For example, when the bike leans over, the contact patch moves to the outside portion of the tire where the circumference is smaller. This is the same as having

All hail the mighty throttle. No other control affects more systems in your bike than this simple little device.

shorter gearing, which raises the number of engine revolutions per minute, or rpm. However, a steady throttle doesn't necessarily accelerate in these situations. In fact, in some turns, the bike can slow down unless you are constantly adding throttle because of the speed lost to wind resistance and tire friction. This is especially true in high-speed turns where straightening out the bike adds enough virtual gearing to require a downshift, even at full throttle settings.

Although you might imagine that the rear suspension would squat as the weight transfers to the rear tire, it, in fact, rises. This is because of the torque reaction on the rear wheel. As you no doubt know from experience, the front suspension also wants to rise when accelerating. That means the bike gets taller under acceleration. For bikes with limited lean-over capability, this can be quite useful in a corner because it adds ground clearance while countering the squatting effects of centrifugal force.

Although you can slowly change direction while being hard on the throttle, quick steering and heavy throttle generally don't mix well because of the aforementioned weight transfer to the rear of the bike. For this

reason, it's best to do any quick flicks before getting hard on the gas, as seen in the diagram on page 62.

When rolling off the throttle, the bike pitches forward, transferring weight to the front tire. Doing this too quickly is a common occurrence even for experienced riders. The faster you roll off, the faster and harder the bike will pitch forward, which can cause all kinds of handling problems if done at an inopportune time. The same can be said for quickly releasing the brakes, which has the same effect as quickly applying the throttle. Combining the last two actions, as many novice sport riders tend to do, makes the bike extremely unstable and "wheelie" prone. The fix for this is to have a transition period where you are doing both actions simultaneously.

One of the important things to remember about suspension is that it works best in the sweet spot, or the middle of its travel range. Being on the throttle in the corners helps the bike stay in this range. Next time you go riding, try the same corner both while coasting through it and while being on the gas. The difference in chassis stability will seem like the difference between night and day. Once you do this comparison, you'll never want to ride through a corner off the gas again.

Anyone who has ever had the pleasure of watching John Kocinski or Freddie Spencer enter a corner and get on the throttle should be familiar with this technique. When Kocinski was racing 250 GP bikes, he could get on the throttle with the grace of a ballet dancer. Back when he was still racing in the AMA nationals, I remember watching him decimate the world's best 250 riders at the 1989 Laguna Seca USGP. I marveled at his ability to get on the throttle so smoothly that I would not have been able to tell when he got back on it had I not been there to hear the engine sound change. That same finesse helped Kocinski win a World Superbike crown on Honda's notoriously finicky RC45.

Spencer arguably had even better control. In his GP days, he was able to charge turns so fast that when the front tire started sliding from being overloaded, he could keep the bike from crashing by *adding* just enough throttle to relieve some pressure so the front tire could regain grip, somehow without high-siding. Using this technique on the three-cylinder Honda NS500, he had his competitors convinced that his bike had better torque coming off the corners than their more powerful four-cylinder bikes. In fact, rumor has it that the memory of those battles was one of the reasons Kenny Roberts chose a three-cylinder engine configuration for his ill-fated Modenas 500 GP bike.

Former World Superbike and 250 GP Champion John Kocinski is famous for his masterful throttle control. His touch was so deft, in fact, that he was able to run markedly more compliant suspension settings than other riders his size because he didn't upset it with excessive throttle movements.

Of course, that kind of riding is not for mere mortals like us. But it does show you what's possible when you combine lots of practice with exceptional sensitivity and reflexes.

Corner Exits

No matter who you are, good throttle control relies on a smoothly operating fuel delivery system. Although it's rare these days to see a carbureted bike with major surging problems, many fuel-injected bikes still struggle with this problem, making it difficult to smoothly get back on the gas. In his *Cycle World* editorial column, "Top Dead Center," Kevin Cameron once noted fuel-injection problems with Matt Mladin's GSX-R750. After repeatedly watching Mladin come through a turn, Cameron noticed the point at which Mladin could get back on the gas was considerably later than the riders of the factory Ducatis he was racing. Cameron hypothesized that this was caused by the fuel-injection system's inability to deliver a small enough quantity of fuel when the throttle was first cracked open, causing a small jerk upon delivery. Because of this, Mladin had to wait until the bike was more vertical so it could handle the hit without seesawing out of control. This is important because going fast, especially on the track, is all about good exit speed.

Exit speed is primarily affected by bike lean. The more the bike is leaned, the less you can apply the throttle. As seen in the chart on page 62 bike lean and throttle opening are negatively correlated. As one goes down, the other goes up due to the finite amount of traction available at any one time. If you find it too difficult to get on the gas early, you're going in too fast and should slow your approach for a faster exit.

The amount of available throttle increases as the bike stands up, but it's better to start sooner and apply it slower than to wait and do it all at once. As mentioned earlier, this is because a smooth, steady increase of throttle keeps the suspension in the sweet spot, whereas a fast application can create additional problems. Taking the time for some specific throttle control practice will help you find the correct rate of throttle application for your bike and riding style.

Practice

It's best to first practice throttle control in a straight line. This can be done almost anywhere. My favorite drills come from Freddie Spencer's High-Performance Riding School. The first drill is to practice rolling on and off the throttle smoothly and slowly. When I say slowly, I mean *very* slowly, especially when rolling off the throttle.

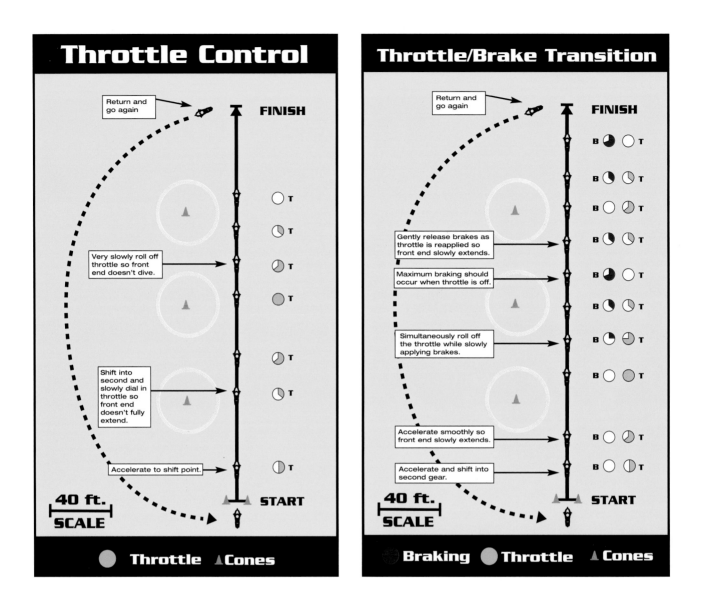

Throttle Control

Return and go again

FINISH

○ T

◑ T

Very slowly roll off throttle so front end doesn't dive.

◑ T

● T

Shift into second and slowly dial in throttle so front end doesn't fully extend.

◑ T

◐ T

Accelerate to shift point.

◑ T

40 ft. SCALE

START

● Throttle ▲ Cones

Throttle/Brake Transition

Return and go again

FINISH

B ◕ ○ T

B ◔ ◔ T

B ○ ◑ T

Gently release brakes as throttle is reapplied so front end slowly extends.

B ◔ ◔ T

Maximum braking should occur when throttle is off.

B ◕ ○ T

B ◔ ◔ T

Simultaneously roll off the throttle while slowly applying brakes.

B ◔ ◔ T

B ○ ◑ T

Accelerate smoothly so front end slowly extends.

B ○ ◑ T

Accelerate and shift into second gear.

B ○ ◑ T

40 ft. SCALE

START

◑ Braking ● Throttle ▲ Cones

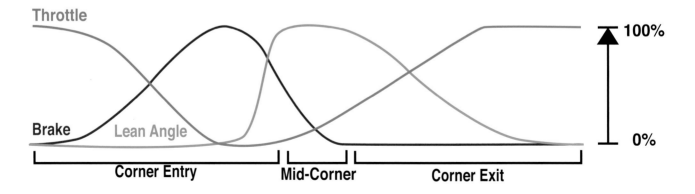

Throttle

Brake   Lean Angle

100%

0%

Corner Entry   Mid-Corner   Corner Exit

This illustration depicts a high-speed turn where the rider is doing a lot of trail braking (see chapter 11) upon entry. Notice how rapidly the bike gets leaned over and how the throttle is being applied before the brakes are completely released. This helps minimize the weight transfer to the rear, which keeps the suspension balanced for better traction during acceleration. As you can see, the application of throttle is inversely proportional to lean angle on exit.

The Spencer method of throttle control mandates rolling off the throttle very slowly while simultaneously applying the brakes during corner entry.

I've found that what most of my students consider slow-ly rolling off the throttle is generally three times faster than it needs to be. It will, in fact, seem painfully slow. You know you are doing it right when the suspension barely moves up and down without any jerkiness. For those of you on fuel-injected BMWs, or any other bike with rough off-idle response, this will be very tricky, but well worth the effort.

After mastering rolling on and off the throttle slowly and smoothly, the next step is to transition back and forth with the brakes. This time, as you slowly roll off the throttle, roll on the brakes. This means that you will be applying varying levels of throttle and brakes *simultane-ously*. This may sound strange, preposterous even, but you will be amazed at how this settles the suspension, keeping the bike from pitching forward and backward. Freddie Spencer won three world championships using this technique, so try it before judging it.

Chapter 10
Shifting

One of the easiest ways to gauge the experience level of a rider is to watch how he shifts. Because shifting is required so often in riding and because sloppy shifting makes the ride uncomfortable, experienced riders learn how to do it by feel. However, even many experienced riders take too much time to shift. Shifting efficiently is important because during the time between shifts, the rider is especially vulnerable. When a sudden change in speed is required, like when a car pulls into your lane, it's vital to be able to accelerate immediately. If you're caught up in the shifting, you won't be able to speed up in an emergency.

Racers, especially drag racers, have turned shifting into an art form. A look at accelerometer data from a race bike reveals an incredibly short amount of time—and speed—is lost in the shifting process. If you're traveling in a straight line, that translates into faster acceleration. In a turn, it means you can hold a steady line and avoid the suspension unloading and the resultant loss of traction and control. If you want to find the optimum shift points for your bike, take it to a shop with a rear-wheel dynamometer. You want the bike to shift at the point where it will enter the next gear at an rpm equal to the engine's torque peak. A list of shops is available online at www.dynojet.com or you can call Dynojet at (800) 992-3525.

Upshifting

Quick, efficient upshifts are pretty easy to master once you take the time to practice the technique. It should be noted, however, that some bikes, like pre-1999 BMWs and Harley-Davidsons, pre-2000 Moto Guzzis, Gold Wings, and all Buells, will never shift well without significant internal and/or external modifications. For this reason, all make poor choices for high-performance riding in stock condition as they cannot be trusted to make reliable shifts mid-corner. Owners of these bikes who don't want to invest in the modifications, some of which are very expensive, will have to plan ahead for shifting. This means being prepared for slower corner speeds and for short shifting, or shifting before the torque peak, so a mid-corner shift is not necessary.

The basic upshifting technique involves preloading the shift lever by pressing your foot down with just slightly less force than that needed to engage the next gear. Next, quickly roll off the throttle approximately 25 percent of its twisting range. When this happens, the torque force on the transmission will temporarily unload, and the preloaded shift lever will now snick into the next gear. For regular shifts at less than full throttle,

Preloading the shift lever with your foot will significantly reduce the amount of time required to shift. On the track that means faster lap times. On the road it means easier transitions between gears for a smoother ride.

a simultaneous, light stab of the clutch will help ease this process. For full-throttle "speed shifting," no clutch is necessary. In fact, it's actually harder on the transmission to use the clutch in this type of situation than to just let the loading forces do the job. Most riders are amazed the first time they find that they don't need to use the clutch in high-performance shifting. These techniques will make the ride noticeably smoother for passengers as well.

Downshifting

High-performance downshifting is a little more difficult than upshifting and requires some significant practice. The most important aspect of downshifting is to match the engine speed with the wheel speed. If the engine speed is too low, the rear wheel will start hopping as it struggles to regain traction, which could result in a nasty crash. This is probably the number one problem novice road racers face when they begin learning to go fast.

The correct technique for downshifting involves turning, or blipping, the throttle about 50 percent of its twisting travel at the instant the clutch is disengaged by pulling in on the lever. Once the clutch is disengaged, the blip will quickly increase engine rpm. When the clutch is re-engaged by letting the lever back out, the new lower gear ratio will require the higher rpm

Shifting

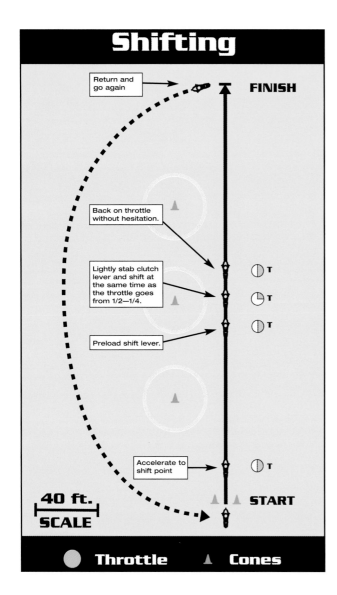

Return and go again

FINISH

Back on throttle without hesitation.

Lightly stab clutch lever and shift at the same time as the throttle goes from 1/2—1/4.

T

T

Preload shift lever.

T

Accelerate to shift point

T

40 ft.
SCALE

START

● **Throttle** ▲ **Cones**

Speed Shifting

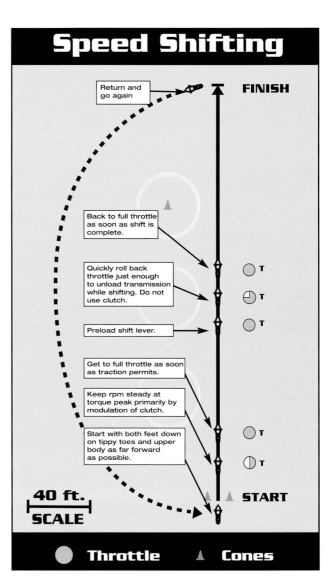

Return and go again

FINISH

Back to full throttle as soon as shift is complete.

Quickly roll back throttle just enough to unload transmission while shifting. Do not use clutch.

T

T

Preload shift lever.

T

Get to full throttle as soon as traction permits.

Keep rpm steady at torque peak primarily by modulation of clutch.

Start with both feet down on tippy toes and upper body as far forward as possible.

T

T

40 ft.
SCALE

START

● **Throttle** ▲ **Cones**

to smoothly blend engine speed to the new rear-wheel speed. Although it's possible to over-blip the throttle in this situation, it's highly unlikely and has little negative effect on the bike. When beginning to learn this technique, you're far better off erring on the side of too much rpm than not enough. By listening carefully to a superbike race at the track or on television, you will hear the blipping of the bikes as they slow down for a corner. GP two-strokes don't do this because they have so little compression by comparison to the four-strokes that they can just bang down gears without worrying about rear-wheel hop. It should be noted that some modern four-strokes are coming with "slipper" clutches that reduce this tendency, making them more forgiving on fast downshifts.

Drag Race Starts

It takes many years of practice to master fast starting and, to make it worse, every bike requires a little different procedure. However, one technique that seems to work for all of them is to start with both feet off the pegs and your weight as far forward as possible. This lets the weight of your legs act like the balancing pole of a tightrope walker, which is especially important on high-horsepower bikes that have a tendency to wheelie. I also like to keep a steady rpm and do most of the work with the clutch. The exact rpm will depend on the bike, and like the shift point, it should be close to the torque peak of the engine. The fewer controls you operate at the same time, the more effective you'll be with each one.

While big wheelies look cool and can be fun, they don't make for fast starts. Ideally, the front wheel should just barely skim the ground. This is the point of highest acceleration where the maximum amount of force is being applied to a given wheelbase and center of gravity. The longer the wheelbase and lower the weight, the more acceleration force can be applied, which is why drag bikes are so long and low. Once the bike begins to wheelie more than a few inches off the ground, additional power makes it want to flip over backwards, rather than accelerate forward. One way to help combat excessive wheelieing on high-horsepower, short-wheelbased sportbikes is to shift early (short-shift) so the engine falls below the torque peak on the next gear.

Like all skills, drag race starts require lots of practice to master, but be mindful of clutch wear. It doesn't take many high-rpm practice starts to destroy a new (or not so new) set of clutch plates. Heat is the enemy here, so let the clutch cool down between runs and it will last much longer.

Chapter 11
Braking

Braking is one of the most misunderstood riding techniques, and there is lots of conflicting data on the subject. On one hand, there are physicists who like to base their theories on mathematical formulas, exploring what is possible. On the other, there are the "experiencialists" whose theories are based on many miles of real-world testing. I fall into the latter category so I will keep the physics to a minimum and concentrate on what has proven to work in the field.

It should also be noted that my techniques and theories are based on extensive testing. This includes performing thousands of scientifically controlled and measured braking runs over a five-year period, from 1995 to 2000, as the editor and test rider for *Motorcycle Consumer News*. During that time, I brake-tested virtually every new bike. Based on the distances achieved when compared to those of other motorcycle publications doing similar work, I would even go so far as to say that I am probably the foremost lay expert in the art in terms of minimum distance and consistency. By testing every bike on the same stretch of asphalt in similar conditions, certain truths emerged.

What Contributes to Quick Stops

Different types of bikes present unique opportunities and liabilities when stopping, though all have to follow

the basic laws of physics. The following is a list of braking "truths" as I have come to know them.

1) *The longer the wheelbase, the shorter the braking distance.* In a quick stop, the forward inertia combined with weight transferring to the front makes the bike want to flip over its front wheel. A longer wheelbase makes the bike a longer lever to resist that force. This is the same reason it is easier to swing a short hammer over your head than a longer one of the same weight.

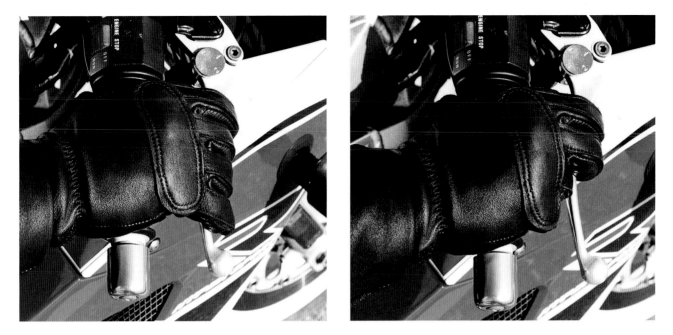

One of the most debated topics in rider training is whether you should use two or four fingers during braking. The correct answer is whichever way you are more comfortable. Most modern-day sportbikes can stand up on the front wheel with only two. However, many cruisers, especially Harley-Davidsons made before 1999, require a whole hand to get any worthwhile stopping power out of the front end.

2) *The lower the center of gravity, or CG, the shorter the braking distance.* Like a longer wheelbase, a lower CG makes it more difficult to flip over. For the same reason, wrestlers try to stay as low as possible to keep their opponents from flipping them over. Although you wouldn't try to lower your riding position on a touring bike or cruiser while braking, how you distribute your luggage, for example, can have a measurable effect on stopping distances. Always store the heavy stuff as low on the bike as possible. If you scoot your body back against the seat of a sportbike, your upper body will naturally get closer to the ground, lowering the combined rider and bike CG. The bike's total weight is much less important than where on the bike that weight is located.

3) *The stickier the tires, the shorter the braking distance.* Traction is what enables a motorcycle's brake system to transform forward momentum into heat. Because of this, racing tires are designed to work best at very high temperatures. That is also what makes them poor choices for street riding as they actually have less traction at lower temperatures than street compound tires. This is not nearly as important with sportbikes as it is with cruisers and tourers. For instance, virtually any modern street tire will allow a sportbike to reach maximum braking force, flipping over forward. However, cruisers and tourers benefit greatly from stickier tires as their long wheelbases normally allow them to lock up the front wheel long before they flip over forward. Of course, softer, stickier tires have a significantly shorter life span, which is why they are not popular on such machines that value high mileage over performance.

4) *The more efficient the braking system, the shorter the braking distance.* Brakes with higher efficiency require less effort at the lever for a given amount of deceleration. The harder you squeeze on the lever during braking, the tighter your muscles become. This can severely limit your dexterity. Relaxed hands and arms have much more feeling, and therefore, they have more control over steering accuracy and brake modulation. Because there is such a huge disparity in braking efficiency between certain models, you need to be careful when riding a new bike for the first time to slowly work up to its limits. For instance, Buell chose to reduce the efficiency of its rear brakes a few years ago. Because many of the riders taking test rides on Buells were Harley-Davidson owners, Buell found that a disproportionate number of them were locking up one or both wheels, often causing a crash. This was because the amount of lever effort they were used to applying on their inefficient bikes was far too strong for modern sportbike brakes.

With the arms holding up most of the weight, the muscles become stressed. This limits dexterity for both steering accuracy and brake modulation.

A vertical back angle means a high center of gravity (CG). The higher and more forward the CG, the more a sportbike wants to flip over its front wheel.

Body slides too far forward up against the tank causing too much weight transfer onto the front end.

A gap between the rear of the seat and the rider indicates he is getting sucked in by the negative G forces.

INCORRECT

A small gap between the gas tank and rider also helps protect the family jewels.

The lower back should be getting a workout helping to hold up the torso. The more work done by the back, the less stress on the arms and hands.

By firmly pressing the knees into the sides of the tank, the rider can keep from sliding forward during hard braking. Endurance racers conserve strength this way.

The little riser on the back of most rider seats provides a nice brace for the rider's rear to push up against.

CORRECT

INCORRECT

CORRECT

Notice the subtle difference in technique in the two pictures above. Both Ducati riders were shot entering the same turn at Daytona. The top picture is of Larry Pegram. His lower body is too far forward and vertical, creating a high center of gravity. This, in turn, causes the rear shock to be fully extended under hard braking. At this point the bike is too close for comfort to flipping over its front wheel. Australian Troy Bayliss, by contrast, keeps his center of gravity low by scooting back on the seat. By clamping his knees on the tank he is able to prevent some deceleration forces from reaching his upper body.

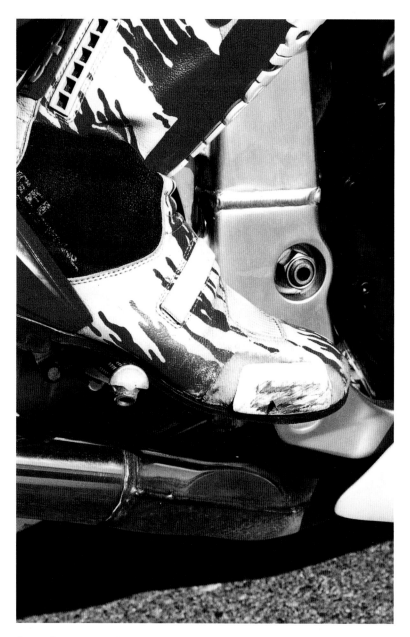

In order to get the best use out of the rear brake, the pedal must be carefully adjusted to the rider. If it's too high it may get activated prematurely or worse, kept on for long periods of time. If it's too low it may require too much "hunting" and "reaching" by the rider to use effectively.

5) *Using both brakes will result in the shortest stopping distance.* The effect of the rear brake depends on the type of bike. Cruisers and tourers both carry a lot of weight on the rear wheels, especially when they have a passenger on board. However, even on a heavily loaded touring rig or a slammed-down cruiser, the rear brake can provide only about 30 percent of the total braking force. That

means if you use only the rear brake to slow down, you are taking a huge safety risk. By contrast, the rear brake on a modern sportbike provides only about 10 percent of the total braking power. On racer-replicas like GSX-Rs and R1s, the percentage is even lower.

During full-power quick stops from 60 miles per hour or more, the rear brake on a sportbike is only good for the first 10 to 15 feet or so, while the weight is fully transitioning onto the front tire. After the first 15 feet, or the first second of traveling time, the rear wheel is off the ground and no amount of rear brake will do anything. If you keep the rear wheel of a modern sportbike on the ground, the stopping distance will be slightly longer than if you have it slightly in the air, but that doesn't mean you shouldn't use the rear brake. Once the rear wheel lifts, the bike becomes very unstable and virtually impossible to steer. At this point, the combined weight of the rider and bike is balancing precariously on the front tire's tiny contact patch. On top of that, the gyroscopic forces of the rear wheel are no longer stabilizing the chassis. This is why racers trade off some ultimate stopping power for more chassis stability by not braking at the bike's absolute maximum capacity. On the track it is much more important to have the chassis settled when entering a turn than to out-brake an opponent. This is because more time is lost regaining stability than is gained by using the brakes. This principle is just as important on the street, where the ability to change direction while braking could mean the difference between life and death.

6) *Modern sport and race bikes are all limited by their wheelbase or center of gravity.* Improving items like the calipers, pads, and tires will not affect the bike's minimum distance potential. In fact, bikes can already flip over forwards when they're using only stock components. However, having said that, non-standard items can improve your chances of flipping. For example, a Harley-Davidson Sportster Sport, by most standards, has mediocre brakes, yet it can stop in a shorter distance than most sport or race bikes. It's not at all easy

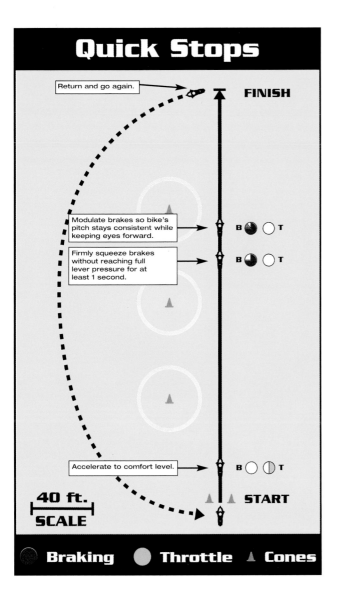

Quick Stops

Return and go again.

FINISH

Modulate brakes so bike's pitch stays consistent while keeping eyes forward.

B ◑ ◯ T

Firmly squeeze brakes without reaching full lever pressure for at least 1 second.

B ◑ ◯ T

Accelerate to comfort level.

B ◯ ◑ T

START

40 ft. SCALE

● **Braking**　● **Throttle**　▲ **Cones**

to do, as it requires Herculean effort at the lever, but it can and has been done. In fact, if cruisers had stickier tires, they would crush sportbikes on the brakes. Right now, the best cruisers stop just as well, and more consistently, than sportbikes. As an example, a Honda Valkyrie or Suzuki Marauder 800 can out-stop every racer-replica made prior to 2000.

Proper Modulation

Now that we understand what makes a bike stop quickly and why, let's go into more detail about how to operate the brakes themselves. Remember, anything that abruptly interferes with the suspension can cause a significant loss of traction. For this reason, it is important to apply the brakes simultaneously and as smoothly as possible.

Applying both brakes simultaneously will help stabilize the chassis and keep it from pitching forward too quickly. Because of the myriad of variables of different bikes and riders, the actual percentage of ideal front to rear braking will depend on the rider's preferences and setup. Experimenting with differing ratios in a controlled environment is the best way to find braking Nirvana on your bike.

The 1998 Honda VFR800FI was the first production motorcycle with a linked front and rear braking system that could actually proportion the brakes better than a skilled rider. Its sophisticated proportioning valves applied just the right amount of front and rear braking for maximum control. In fact, John Kocinski won a World Superbike Championship on an RC45 with a similar system installed. Unfortunately, many of the other Hondas with linked brakes never found that magic combination, so the system never took off as a feature.

When using the brakes, be sure not to apply them too quickly. This is a common mistake of both novice and experienced riders. When this happens, the rear wheel is prone to skidding, and the front end will dive rapidly, causing major instability. A good measure of proper application is minimal suspension movement. You can easily feel how much downward pitch the bike goes through during braking. As described in chapter 9, "Fast Freddie" Spencer pioneered a technique for minimizing suspension movement by slowly applying the brakes while still rolling out of the throttle. That meant there were short periods of time where he was applying both at the same time. This makes the throttle/brake transition as smooth as possible, which leaves the largest amount of suspension travel available for absorbing bumps while entering a turn.

Antilock Brake Systems, Linked and Integrated Brakes

Motorcycles often fall down if the brakes are locked up for too long. For this reason, most bikes let you choose the appropriate amount of braking for either end. However, we're seeing more and more enhancements these days to the original formula of two separate systems for front and rear. As previously mentioned, I really like the sophisticated linked brakes of the VFR800FI, but I haven't been too thrilled with any of the others. I really don't like the integrated brakes of the GL1500 Gold Wing or any of the Moto Guzzis with this system. Integrated brakes on these models apply the rear caliper and one front caliper whenever the rear brake lever is applied. This can become a problem on wet or slick,

Trail braking while entering a corner reduces the bike's rake and trail, enabling it to turn quicker and easier. It can, however, easily cause a lock-up and crash if you're not careful. Here, Doug Chandler trail brakes into a corner at Daytona with perfect form. You can tell he's trail braking by looking at the combination of lean angle and compressed forks on his machine.

gravel roads where too much front brake can cause a lockup, yet the rear is needed to slow the bike down.

On the other hand, an antilock brake system, or ABS, can be a tremendous advantage in treacherous, low-traction situations. It's becoming standard equipment on more and more automobiles these days, and I

predict the same will happen with bikes in the future. Generally speaking, you give up some ultimate dry performance, but it's more than made up for with the dramatically improved, wet weather performance. It's rare that that last bit of braking performance is likely to be a consideration on dry roads, unless you're racing, and race bikes don't use ABS. The BMW K1200RS actually works superbly in both conditions. That shows the potential for this technology, which is only going to improve. Even with the premium price of today's systems, they are well worth the money.

Trail Braking

Motorcycle students are usually taught to do all of the braking before making a turn. This is generally good advice, but there are times when it is necessary, or even preferable, to brake while entering a corner. This is commonly known as trail braking. Under braking, a forward weight transfer causes the front end to "dive." This has the effect of reducing the rake and trail of the machine, which makes it want to turn quicker and with less effort. The benefits are obvious when trying to corner quickly. But it is a difficult skill to master and should be learned by gradually working up to a quick pace. Here again, the Spencer technique of slowly rolling on the throttle while simultaneously slowly releasing the brakes will keep the front end from "pogoing" up, allowing the traction to remain as consistent as possible. Trail braking is not the same as braking once you are already in a corner. That has the opposite effect and actually makes the bike want to stand up. The specific point at which you release the brakes is less important than making sure that the release is slow and controlled.

When Brakes Lock Up

For a motorcyclist, few things are as scary as a front wheel locking up under braking. Rear wheel skids are also unnerving, but they are a bit easier to manage. In the event of a rear wheel skid, you can maintain your line by leaving the wheel locked up while steering into the turn or by gently letting up on the rear lever and immediately reapplying it once the tire has regained traction. Of course, it's important to remember that if you let up too quickly, the bike is at risk of hurling you into the air in a "high side." This can happen when the rear wheel violently regains traction, turning the sideways inertia into flipping power.

Rear wheel locks can certainly be challenging, but front wheel locks are even more dangerous because they allow very little time to react, making it difficult to prevent a crash. You can address front wheel lock up by releasing the lever as soon and as smoothly as possible. This will help the wheels' gyroscopic forces and the chassis' trail to regain control. The bike will want to stand up straight, but when it does this, it will end up pointing in the direction the front tire is facing when it regains traction. As a result, you may need to make an immediate steering correction. Next, slowly reapply the brakes. With the forks fully extended at this point, a quick stab at the lever will cause a major compression in the forks, creating additional control problems.

I do not think it is possible to practice panic stops. In panic situations, your body reacts by doing only what it's used to doing without the conscious thought of technique. Only by practicing good technique on a regular basis will it become second nature to you and, therefore, be available when you need it most. Perhaps the most important thing to remember in a panic situation is that your heightened adrenaline level will cause you to squeeze the brake lever harder than you typically do. So, when applying the brakes in a panic stop, force yourself to limit the amount of pressure you're exerting.

Chapter 12
Body
Positioning

As I mentioned earlier, where you position your body on the bike has a profound impact on how it will handle. It also determines how much physical effort you will need to control the bike. According to Zen Master Dogen, the ability to execute the correct posture during meditation practice is itself considered to be enlightenment. Although I can't promise you a mystical experience, by practicing what I call my "Ten Steps to Proper Cornering," your body and bike will begin to flow in a rhythmic harmony more akin to ballet than alligator wrestling.

Movement Efficiency

If you apply the Ten Steps while riding, you will learn to give the bike only what it needs to complete the task at hand. This "movement efficiency" process is similar to that experienced by professional dancers and fighters as they learn to conserve their strength rather than wasting it on excessive muscle tension or extraneous movements.

I was introduced to the concept of movement efficiency during my martial arts training, which I began as a way to help my road racing skills. I learned that by completely relaxing the muscles that weren't absolutely necessary for a given action and instead focusing my

energy on those that were, I could maintain my strength for extended periods of time and be much more powerful with each action. Each of the martial arts techniques maximizes your body's natural leveraging abilities to get the most bang for your muscles' buck. Just for kicks, I still enjoy using this process on those "ring-the-bell" games at fairs. By focusing and leveraging, I'm usually

Outside arm is tense because it pulls on the bars for steering. This keeps the rider from leaning with the bike.

Looking straight ahead instead of through turn.

Rider centerline is to the outside of bike centerline.

Outside arm is relaxed and not fighting for control with inside arm.

Looking through the turn to exit point while keeping head perpendicular to the road.

INCORRECT

CORRECT

Inside foot tucked up and out of the way.

Inside arm is doing all the steering.

Rider centerline is to the inside of bike centerline.

Outside arm is tense because it pulls on the bars for steering. This keeps the rider from leaning with the bike.

Looking straight ahead instead of through turn.

Rider centerline is to the outside of bike centerline.

Outside arm is relaxed and not fighting for control with inside arm.

Looking through the turn to exit point while keeping head perpendicular to the road.

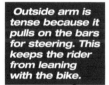

INCORRECT

Inside foot sticking out too far from footpeg.

CORRECT

Inside foot tucked up and out of the way.

Inside arm is doing all the steering.

Rider centerline is to the inside of bike centerline.

CORRECT

CORRECT

INCORRECT

Great, good, and bad: Three World Superbike riders exit turn two at Laguna Seca with three different body positions. Noriyuki Haga (top) demonstrates picture perfect form as he hangs off with his signature style. His posture is aggressive yet relaxed as he lets gravity do much of the turning work. He also does a fantastic job of looking through the turn to his exit point. Colin Edwards (middle) also displays good form with his centerline to the inside of the bike's centerline (though not as much as Haga), his outside arm resting on the tank and a good view of his exit point. Larry Pegram (bottom) looks like he's riding a dirt tracker more than a road racer. His centerline is on the wrong side of the bike's centerline as he pushes his Ducati underneath him, squandering ground clearance. He's also looking straight ahead instead of at the corner exit and has a tense outside arm. You'd be tense too if you were riding at that speed and couldn't see more than 20 feet in front of you!

able to hit harder than guys who are significantly stronger than I am.

Chassis Dynamics

The first thing to understand about body positioning is that the motorcycle's chassis is engineered so that it will go around corners quickly and smoothly. Adding a rider into the mix interferes with the bike's inherent abilities. The job of a rider is to become as "invisible" as possible. In other words, although you can't help but interfere with the bike, the trick is to interfere with it in a skillful manner.

The idea that a bike is better without a rider was most clearly demonstrated to me several years ago as I was shooting photos inside turn one at Daytona International Speedway. In 600cc Supersport action, Yoshimura Suzuki's Aaron Yates was running in third place when his front end let go while he was hard on the brakes. Although he went down, the impact from the crash bounced the bike back up on its wheels, and the riderless GSX-R600 passed Miguel DuHamel and another rider into the lead. Of course, it soon fell over as there was no longer anyone controlling it, but the event clearly demonstrated how well bikes can work without the interference of a rider.

Crucial Comfort

Some of my cornering tips will seem a little awkward at first, but after you practice them enough, they will all become second nature. However, because every rider's body is unique, the application of each technique will look slightly different depending on the rider's flexibility, fitness level, etc. This is why two gymnasts performing the exact same routines can be awarded completely different scores for style. When practicing the Ten Steps, I encourage you to find your own unique style. Your style will primarily be dictated by what feels comfortable to you. Each step has a certain amount of leeway, and your style will be the result of how you interpret the movement. For example, notice the different styles of Colin Edwards and Noriyuki Haga on page 78 as they follow the Ten Steps on the same turn. Although their styles differ, both are correct. By contrast, Larry Pegram breaks several of the rules doing it "his way" with less impressive results. This is not to say he isn't fast, but he is certainly working harder and has been less consistent in competition.

I've heard several racers, and even riding instructors, talk about the importance of weighting the outside peg during cornering. However, my personal experience and that of my students has shown that it doesn't matter how much weight you put on the outside verses inside peg so long as you're in a comfortable riding position. In fact, there are many published photos of GP star Randy Mamola clearly showing his outside foot completely off the peg during cornering. Given that he has beaten some of the best riders in the world, it obviously isn't a requirement to weight the outside peg to go fast. Of course, if you are more comfortable doing it then, by all means, weight it as much as you like.

The most important aspect of proper technique is to position your body in as natural a way as possible while still following the rules. You should never use excessive muscle force to stretch your body into a particular position. For instance, if you are going to be dragging your knee, let it drop down in whatever position is comfortable. You don't ever want to "try" to touch your knee. If you do the technique properly, it will happen all by itself when your speed warrants it. On the other hand, if you are riding a cruiser or tourer and don't want to radically hang off the bike, simply do the minimum necessary to follow the rules, and you will still significantly improve your ability to control the bike.

Keep in mind that some muscles, like those in your lower back, will probably require some strengthening before you can do the technique properly. Because it's critical to have a relaxed upper body, your lower back and thighs will be a little stressed until they get used to holding up more weight than normal.

There are two reasons why it is so important to have a relaxed upper body. First off, the more stressed your muscles are, the less dexterity they have. To illustrate this, take a pen and sign your name three times on a piece of paper in the usual way. Notice how your hand effortlessly flows from one letter to the next with repeatable accuracy. Next, tighten your grip and flex your forearm as hard as you can. Sign your name three more times while maintaining the muscle tension. Notice how difficult it is to maintain control of the pen and how each of these signatures looks totally different. Your ability to control your motorcycle is just like being able to control your pen. A relaxed upper body makes it possible to change direction or speed with repeatable accuracy.

The second reason for having a relaxed upper body is that this will allow the bike to do its necessary low-amplitude weaving. If your upper body is rigidly trying to control the steering, the bike's need to slightly wiggle the front wheel in order to maintain a "smooth" line is compromised, which will cause it to run wide as the wiggles grow larger to compensate.

10 Steps to Proper Cornering

Step 1: Reposition foot

No matter what kind of bike you ride, ground clearance will become an issue as your skill and speed increase. Whether you're using footpegs or floorboards, it's important to tuck in your foot so it doesn't stick out. Otherwise, it can catch on the ground and throw your leg back hard enough to cause you to crash.

Step 2: Pre-position body

To keep the bike stable while entering turns, it is important not to upset the suspension. The best way to avoid upsetting the suspension is to pre-position your body in your final cornering pose before you enter the turn. This way, the weight transfer happens when your suspension is perpendicular to the ground. This is the best position for the suspension to deal with it. The important rule here is to keep the centerline of your upper body to the inside of your bike's centerline. It doesn't matter if it is an inch or a foot to the inside so long as it's to the inside and that the distance to the inside remains constant throughout the turn. For example, if you move your upper body's centerline six inches to the inside of the bike's centerline, stay six inches to the inside no matter what lean angle you are at, and don't move back to center until the bike is completely vertical again. By moving your body into the inside airstream, the high-pressure area created by doing so (especially when dropping a knee out), will give the bike a pivot point to steer around. This further lessens the amount of force needed at the bars to steer.

Step 3: Push on outside grip

As soon as you pre-position your body, the bike will want to fall to the inside of the turn. To prevent this, you need to push on the outside grip to keep the bike on a straight path. The bike will look a little strange at this point as it will be traveling straight but leaning to the outside. This is because the outward lean is necessary to counter the gravitational force trying to pull your off-center body to the ground.

Step 4: Locate turn point

Once your body is in position, you must quickly choose a reference point to mark your turn-in. If you are practicing, it can be a well-positioned cone. On the road, it might be a spot on the pavement, a rock, or a tree just off the street or even an imaginary coordinate as you might use in billiards to bank a ball. It's best to use something that will allow you to easily sense its position since you will not be looking directly at it when you start the turn.

Step 5: Look through turn

After choosing your turn point, you should look as far through the turn as possible to find your exit point. If the turn is set up in such a way that you cannot see the exit, look to the farthest point you can locate, and keep modifying your view until you can see the exit.

Step 6: Relax outside grip

When you have reached your turn point, release the pressure on the outside grip. This will allow gravity to help pull your off-center body and the bike into the turn.

Step 7: Push on inside grip

At the same time you release the pressure on your outside grip, add pressure to the inside grip until your desired lean angle is achieved. It's very important to do this as quickly and smoothly as possible. Once you have reached your desired lean angle, use only the inside arm to make all of the steering corrections by pushing or pulling. The reason for this is to keep your two arms from wrestling for control over the bike's steering. The bike must be allowed to use its trail and gyroscopic processional forces to continually re-balance itself at your desired lean angle. By pushing and pulling with only one arm, you allow enough "give" in the system for the bike to do what it needs to do to keep balanced and hold a smooth, tight line. The more you use both arms to steer, the wider and more jagged your line will become, requiring even more effort at the bars to maintain a given radius. Of course, the outside arm should still be holding on, but it should be completely relaxed and ready in case it is needed. On a sport or race bike, it's best to rest your outside arm on the tank to preserve strength and make sure it's not trying to steer the motorcycle. On a cruiser or tourer, your outside elbow should be pointing down and your outside shoulder muscles should be completely relaxed.

Warning: When trying this technique for the first time, your bike will be able to turn so much more efficiently that you will be at risk of running off the inside of the corner. Make sure you try it at a slower speed or where there is plenty of inside run-off until you get used to your bike's newfound turning ability.

Step 8: Roll on throttle

Once the bike's suspension has settled into the turn, you should get back on the throttle as early and smoothly as possible. Getting the initial "crack" of the throttle open is the most critical part. Remember that the lean angle will limit the amount of throttle that can be applied, so only accelerate as hard as the bike's lean angle will allow. For example, at full lean only a little throttle can be applied before the rear tire runs out of traction. On the other hand, full throttle may be applied when the bike is completely upright. Everything else falls along that continuum, and the rate of throttle application should mimic the rate of straightening up. Trying to accelerate at too much of a lean angle or turning the throttle too quickly at any particular angle is a recipe for a slide out. Accelerating out of a turn will also help pick the bike up, requiring less force on the bars to get upright.

Step 9: Push outside grip

To help the throttle get the bike upright when exiting a turn, countersteer in the opposite direction by pushing on the outside grip or pulling on the inside grip. It is important that you not pull your body up to the bike's centerline while countersteering back.

Step 10: Move back to neutral

Most riders have a strong urge to move their bodies back to a neutral position in the center of the bike too early in the corner exit. It's best to wait until the bike is completely, or almost completely, upright before doing so. This is especially true when accelerating hard as the available traction will be used up primarily with the throttle, and any large body weight shifts could upset the suspension, squandering any remaining traction.

Continued from page 79

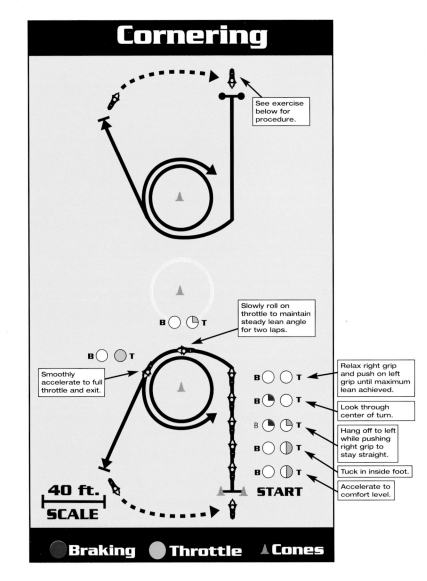

Cornering

See exercise below for procedure.

Slowly roll on throttle to maintain steady lean angle for two laps.

Smoothly accelerate to full throttle and exit.

Relax right grip and push on left grip until maximum lean achieved.

Look through center of turn.

Hang off to left while pushing right grip to stay straight.

Tuck in inside foot.

Accelerate to comfort level.

40 ft.
SCALE

START

●**Braking** ●**Throttle** ▲**Cones**

Motocross bikes require the opposite technique of street bikes. On a dirt bike, the rider pushes the bike underneath him, instead of leaning with the bike.

Transitions

Transitioning between multiple curves such as tight switchbacks and esses requires a slight modification to the Ten Steps. Instead of completely finishing one turn and then preparing for the next, the preparation for the second turn starts happening while still in the first turn. As the bike is exiting but still leaned over from the original turn, quickly but smoothly move your body into the proper position for the next turn, then continue with the rest of the steps.

I find it's best to practice transitions by setting up figure-eight turns in a large parking lot. You should be able to smoothly flow from one turn to the next without any sudden throttle changes. If you work at it, your throttle position won't change at all as you do the figure eight. Doing figure-eight turns is a great exercise because it combines virtually all of the skills taught in this book, and doesn't give you a headache like going in circles over and over again can. Once you get good at figure-eight turns, the Ten Steps will become second nature.

When transitioning between two tight corners it's necessary to shift your body to the opposite side of the bike before the first turn is actually complete. When that happens, for a short period of time the bike will still be leaning toward the first turn as you pre-position your body for the second. If you don't do this, you will be forced to make a serious weight transfer while steering, which will upset the suspension and possibly cause a loss of traction.

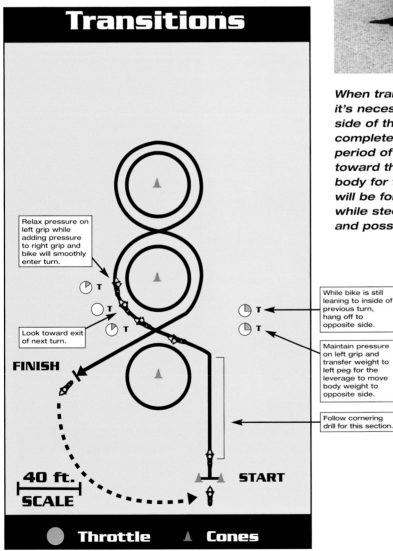

Transitions

Relax pressure on left grip while adding pressure to right grip and bike will smoothly enter turn.

Look toward exit of next turn.

While bike is still leaning to inside of previous turn, hang off to opposite side.

Maintain pressure on left grip and transfer weight to left peg for the leverage to move body weight to opposite side.

Follow cornering drill for this section.

FINISH

40 ft.
SCALE

START

● Throttle ▲ Cones

Chapter 13
Low-Speed U-Turns

Few activities in street riding are as frustrating as having to make a low-speed, tight turn in a limited amount of space—especially if you don't know the technique. I always teach this skill last in my Advanced Riding Clinics because it requires using the exact opposite technique than the one used in higher speed cornering, and I don't like to confuse people. Fortunately, it is one of the easiest skills to learn. In fact, most riders are able to reduce their minimum turning diameter by 30 to 40 percent in as little as five minutes of practice!

As mentioned earlier, besides the length of the wheelbase there are two primary factors that affect a bike's turning ability: steering angle and lean angle. Because anyone can turn the handlebars to the stops, increasing lean angle is the basis for real improvements.

Increasing Lean Angle

In high-speed turns, you want to conserve as much lean angle as possible. Conversely, in tight U-turns you purposely

Shift body position as far to the outside as the inside arm length will alow. The crotch should ride as far up and to the tank as possible.

Look at the ground as far behind you as possible to keep the turn tight.

Weight the outside peg to maintain balance. It is the primary load carrier during tight U-turns.

The real work in tight turns is done with the inside arm, which must vary pressure to both steer the bike and keep it balanced. Right turns are more difficult because that hand must control the throttle simultaneously.

CORRECT

Even heavy, full-dress tourers can make almost effortless tight turns with the proper technique. Note that the rider's inside foot is completely off the peg. With the majority of the rider's weight on the outside peg, the inside leg is just along for the ride.

want to use up as much lean angle as possible. The reason for keeping some lean angle available on high-speed turns is to be able to have a reserve in case the suspension needs to compress due to a road irregularity or a rider input. If there is no lean angle in reserve when the bike hits a bump, something hard, like a footpeg, a floorboard, or an exhaust pipe, will hit the pavement, possibly bouncing the bike off its tires. In low-speed tight turns, on the other hand, this type of hazard does not exist, so you can use the maximum amount of lean angle to make turns as sharply as possible.

In order to really lean a bike over, you must counter the effect of gravity so the bike doesn't fall down. In high-speed corners, this is done primarily with centrifugal force. In low-speed corners, however, centrifugal force is not enough. It's important to reposition the weight of your body to counterbalance the bike's weight. The way to do this is by moving as much weight as possible to the opposite side of the turn. This is similar to catamaran sailors hanging their bodies off the side of their boats to keep them from flipping over. Of course, this is exactly the opposite of what you've been learning about high-performance cornering in this book, so it's important to use this technique only when making low-speed U-turns and the like.

The key to making this technique work is learning to trust that the bike will not fall over when properly counter-balanced so you can relax your grip on the bars. Just as in high-speed cornering, it's best to make all the steering inputs with the inside arm. By relaxing the outside arm, it will be considerably easier to maintain a tight line because the two arms will not be wrestling one another for control of the handlebars.

By moving your body to the opposite side of the bike, the majority of your weight will be on the outside footpeg. Again, this is exactly the opposite process of that used in high-speed cornering. It's important to move your crotch area as far up and out on the tank as possible to find the ideal balance point. The farther away from the bike you can move your body, the more lean angle you will be able to generate, and the tighter turn you will achieve.

The one thing that will make or break low-speed turns is your vision. Where you look has a profound impact on where you go. In order to have the tightest turn possible, look behind you and at the ground, and the bike will follow your lead with a clean, tight line.

A great way to practice low-speed U-turns is by making gradually tighter circles in a parking lot. This lets you gradually work up to your minimum diameter at your own pace. Try each side separately until you are comfortable with both sides. When you have mastered this, you can start riding a figure-eight pattern so you won't get as dizzy as you can get doing circles. Like all skills, the more you practice, the easier the techniques become. And if you master the exercise, you'll never dread another tight U-turn again.

Preventing the Fall

Perhaps the biggest obstacle to overcome when making tight U-turns is the fear of falling over. If the bike starts leaning to the point where you're afraid the steering can't keep it from falling down, all you need to do is dial in some more throttle. This will make the bike want to stand up, using the same centrifugal force that keeps racers from falling down at extreme lean angles. As the old adage goes, "When in doubt, gas it!"

Chapter 14
Riding
Two-up

Sport riding two-up is not as common as riding solo, but it can be just as rewarding when both participants are skilled. This is especially true when the two riders have lots of experience riding together as a team. High-performance, two-up riding is just like dancing: One partner leads, the other follows, and together they work like a single moving part. I've seen many a skilled pair ride right around unsuspecting solo riders who thought they were really moving. Seeing a really experienced pair ride as one is a truly beautiful sight. After all, part of the fun of riding is sharing the experience with others. That's why we join clubs and have riding buddies. Just as in dancing, the secret to good two-up riding is rhythm. That means knowing the right moves and executing them in the proper sequence with precise timing. When done properly, the motorcycle will operate smoothly.

A passenger's added weight and wind resistance can't help but affect the bike's handling and suspension. Knowing this, the goal of a good passenger is to position her body in a way that will minimize that effect as much as possible. The way in which to do this varies depending on what the bike is doing at the moment. We will cover proper passengering techniques for each of the main bike states as they relate to high-performance riding. But first we must go over some passengering basics.

Priscilla Knows Passengering

My favorite passenger is a woman named Priscilla Wong who happens to be blessed with natural talent for two-up riding. Although she weighs 140 pounds, Priscilla affects the chassis less than many 110-pound passengers. The first time I took her for a ride was when I was magazine testing a Buell S3 at the Buttonwillow racetrack. I told Priscilla I would start slowly and that she should tap me on the shoulder to let me know when I started going too fast. I was amazed at how well she could follow my lead, and within two laps we were scraping hard parts in almost every turn—even with us both hanging off the inside—yet we never missed a beat. By lap three, she was giving me the "go faster" thumbs-up sign. Unfortunately, and surprisingly, we were already at the limits of the bike.

I asked Priscilla how she was able to have such composure during those touchy moments. She explained that she had total trust in my abilities, which allowed her to concentrate on simply being a good passenger without having to worry about the bike's limits—that was my job. Later I realized the profundity of her words. After all, any doubt she had would have negatively affected the ride. The best thing for a passenger, or rider, for that matter, to do is to act out of total trust and not let fear impede the bike's abilities. Faith is the key to keeping fear at bay so you can ride

Super-passenger Priscilla Wong says the most important factors in high-performance passengering are "complete trust in the rider" and "going with the flow."

Here Priscilla demonstrates riding two-up with the author at a serious lean angle. Even at this speed she finds the calm to ham it up for the camera.

Leaning way over to get a view of the road ahead causes aerodynamic and weight-distribution problems.

While it may seem harmless, a closed hand can become a painful "gutbuster" during a quick stop.

Bracing against the rider's mid or upper back during braking puts excessive pressure on his upper body.

It's important to not unevenly weight the pegs, especially during cornering, braking, or accelerating.

INCORRECT

The "one-eyed peek" is the best way for a passenger to see what's up ahead without upsetting the bike's handling.

In this position, a quick flip of the wrist angles a passenger's hands for going or stopping.

By placing the arms around the rider, a little squeeze can help stabilize a passenger against various G-forces.

Bracing against the tank is the best way to keep pressure off the rider during quick stops.

CORRECT

at your best. Priscilla also said that trust happens before getting on the bike. If she didn't trust the rider, she wouldn't get on the bike in the first place. She told me, "Riding on the back of a motorcycle is a lot like riding a roller coaster. If I ever start to feel a little scared, I just imagine I'm on a roller coaster ride and relax and enjoy the ride."

Choosing Appropriate Companions

There are many things to take into consideration when deciding if you should take a ride with someone. You should never accept a ride from anyone who drinks and rides. Furthermore, you should refuse to ride with anyone who has a history of crashes or a *laissez faire* attitude toward them. You should never ride with someone who does not wear appropriate safety gear including a DOT-approved helmet. And finally, you should never ride with anyone you do not trust completely. Without trust, you will not be comfortable enough to relax and go with the flow of riding. If you lack trust, you are putting both yourself and the rider at risk because a passenger who is afraid and stiff will make jerky movements that can greatly upset chassis stability.

Riders should choose their passengers using similar criteria. As a rider, your rules should be "No sobriety, no gear, no service." Remember, just as your passengers

When boarding, swinging the right leg completely over the seat is the least taxing on the rider. If that is not possible, the rider should counter the passenger's weight by leaning the bike slightly away from her as she puts her left foot on the left peg, stands up and swings the right leg over the bike. By leaning forward the rider makes it easier for the passenger to climb on the bike. The passenger should never put her feet down again until it's time to get off.

are putting their lives in your hands, you are putting your life in their hands as well, so make sure your passengers are worthy of that level of trust.

Before the Ride

Once you've decided to accept the responsibility of carrying a passenger, there must be an agreement about which behaviors are considered "acceptable risks." The range of risks passengers are willing to accept is broad, so proper communication up front is essential to avoiding a problem on the road. Before beginning the ride, both rider and passenger should also agree on some hand or body signals to use while riding. These will be useful for communicating whether the pace is too fast or too slow. Signals can even express the need for a bathroom break. As the rider, it is your responsibility to make sure the passenger has brought proper riding gear. If they lack proper gear, you should be able to provide him or her with it. The same rules of riding gear apply for the passenger as they do for the rider. See chapter 20 for a full explanation of proper riding gear.

Getting On and Off

Once both the rider and the passenger are comfortable with one another's skills and attitude, and have agreed on some ground rules, it's time to have some fun. Although getting on and off may not seem like a big deal, I've seen many a bike go down due to a lack of communication or poor technique.

As the rider, the first step is to indicate that you are ready, which is best done verbally. At this point, you should balance the bike, and direct the passenger to approach from the left side. Once you have acknowledged that you are ready for the passenger, the passenger should put his or her left hand on your shoulder as a signal that he or she is about to climb on board. Then, your passenger should use either of the techniques shown in the photos to get on. Once on board, the passenger should acknowledge that he or she is in place and ready to go.

Monkey See, Monkey Do

Once underway, the passenger's job is to be as unobtrusive as possible. The best way to accomplish this is to have the passenger mimic your movements as closely as possible. If you lean 20 degrees to the left, your passenger should lean 20 degrees to the left. If you tuck down, your passenger should tuck down. One of the worst things for a passenger to do is lean or move in the opposite direction of the rider.

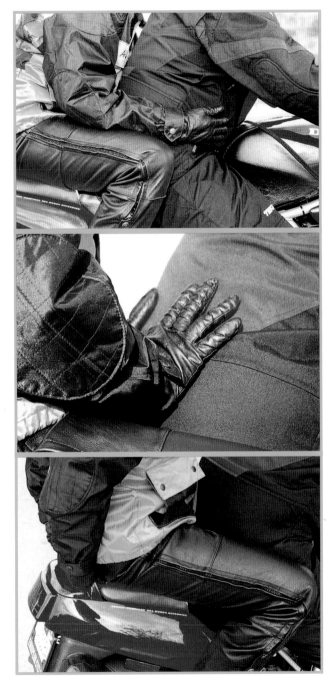

During braking, if you can't reach around the rider and use the tank as a brace, there are several other acceptable alternatives for your hands: Holding the rider's waist/hips (top), placing your hands on the rider's lower back (center), or holding onto a grab rail (bottom).

After a certain amount of time in the saddle, the passenger's knees, ankles, and butt will get sore and will need to be moved to keep proper blood flow to these areas. It is the passenger's responsibility to make these adjustments slowly and at non-critical times, like on a straightaway, when such movement won't be disturbing to the rider.

Accelerating and Braking

The physics involved with adding a passenger to a motorcycle necessitates some changes in riding style. With all the added weight to the rear of the bike, acceleration has a tendency to make the front end extremely light, especially when going uphill. Big-bore sport bikes, and even many middleweights, become impossible to accelerate at full throttle without "wheelying." This reduces traction and also causes the forks to extend, which slows down the steering by changing the bike's rake and trail. These two effects cause the bike to take a wider line in a corner at a given speed. In other words, when taking a passenger, you will have to slow down to maintain your "normal" line.

The added passenger mass will require a lot more braking force to slow down and can cause a larger weight transfer to the front. This means you need to leave significantly more room for stopping than you usually do. This is not something you want to find out by accident. On the positive side, the rear brake will have additional effectiveness because of the rearward weight bias.

Passengers are most often thrown out of balance during acceleration and braking. It's helpful for your passenger to be familiar with your throttle and braking habits. By making your passenger comfortable, you can prevent a lot of anxious moments, not to mention annoying helmet bonks. In order to keep from falling off the back of the bike or sliding forward into the rider, the passenger needs to be anchored to the bike and to you.

As the legs are the strongest muscles of the human body, it's best for them to do as much of the work as possible. Depending on a bike's particular setup, the passenger should dig her heels or toes into the sides of the footpeg brackets or frame to have a solid connection with the bike. Additionally, she can use her thighs to stabilize herself by putting a little squeeze on the rider.

Passengers' hands can be positioned in several different ways. For acceleration forces, passengers should keep their hands forward where they can hold on to something. Their hands can be on the sides of the rider's hips or in front of his abdomen, but they should always gently "hold onto," rather than "dig

When accelerating hard with a passenger, the bike unweights the front tire much more than normal and may even wheelie. Any attempt at steering during such times is a real roll of the dice as traction is at a minimum.

into," the rider. The hands can also rest on the tank while the passenger gently squeezes the rider with the sides of her arms to help keep herself in place.

Deceleration forces are best handled by either bracing against the gas tank or holding onto the passenger grab rails if the bike is so equipped. Passengers can also brace themselves against the rider, but it's very important that they do so on as low a point on the rider's back as possible. If the passenger puts her hands too high up on the rider, it will cause a dangerous amount of pressure on the rider's upper body and hands, which will make it very difficult for him to modulate the brakes effectively.

Cornering

The added weight of a passenger compresses the suspension, significantly reducing a bike's ground clearance and, therefore, decreasing the cornering speed. Although stiffer suspension settings, springs, and tire pressures will help, a speed reduction of at least 30 percent is needed to maintain the same safety level as riding without a passenger.

It's natural to want to see what's ahead, but passengers should not move their heads more than is necessary. This is because the shift in weight distribution combined with the aerodynamic effects of a helmet in the wind can cause the motorcycle to unexpectedly lean and turn. Generally, the rider can make up for small changes in these areas, but a quick, sudden change can cause major instability. That is why passengers need to minimize any movements on the bike that are not in sync with the rider, especially when dealing with weighting the footpegs. When Freddie Spencer takes students around a racetrack as part of his high-performance riding school, he uses an effective technique to get his passenger to lean in the proper direction. He asks his

Looking inside the turn helps passengers plan for what's ahead. They should also mimic the rider's lean in turns.

passenger to look over his right shoulder in a right-hand turn and to look over his left shoulder in a left-hand turn. This ensures that the passenger positions his or her body so that the mass of body weight is located on the inside of the turn.

"I like to stay on the balls of my feet so I'm ready to reposition my weight in sync with the rider," says Wong. "Give the rider as much freedom and space as possible, but lightly keep in constant physical contact with him so you can feel his movements and react instantaneously. Be very aware of what the rider is doing and what his needs are. The more you ride with a specific rider, the easier it is to predict his movements. When you get good enough at this, cornering two-up can be as graceful as a ballet."

Chapter 15
Suspension Setup

Having the right suspension setup is one of the keys to riding fast and safely. No matter which shock or fork you have, they all require proper adjustment to work to their maximum potential. We covered basic suspension theory in chapter 3. Now it's time to learn how to specifically set up the components. If you follow my suggested procedures, you can make remarkable improvements in your bike's handling.

Adjusting Static Spring Sag

The first step is to set the sag and determine if you have the correct-rate springs. Static sag is the distance the suspension compresses between being fully topped-out and fully loaded. This is measured with the rider on board in a riding position. Static sag is also referred to as "static ride height" or "race sag." If you've ever measured sag before, you may have noticed that you can check it three or four times and get three or four different numbers, even when you haven't changed anything. The reason this happens is due to friction in the forks, shocks, or linkage. Fortunately, Race Tech's Paul Thede developed a method for sag measurement that takes friction into account. We'll start by setting the sag for the rear suspension.

Rear Suspension

Step 1: Extend the suspension completely by getting the rear wheel off the ground. Sometimes it helps to have a few friends around to accomplish this task. Bikes with centerstands can usually be rocked up on the stand to unload the suspension. Make sure that you're careful when doing this. Most road race stands will not work because the suspension will still be loaded by resting on the swing-arm rather than the wheel. Using a measuring tape, calculate the distance from the axle vertically to some point on the chassis. In my opinion, metric measurements are easiest to use. When measuring, try to hold the tape measure as close to vertical as possible as this will produce the most accurate measurement. This measurement is called "L1." Record the L1 measurement, as this number will be used as a reference point later in the process (figure 1).

Step 2: Remove the bike from the stand and put the rider on board in a riding position. Have a third person balance the bike from the front. For proper accuracy, you must take into account the friction of the suspension linkage. This is where Thede's procedure is different from the standard method of measurement. Next, push the rear end down about 25

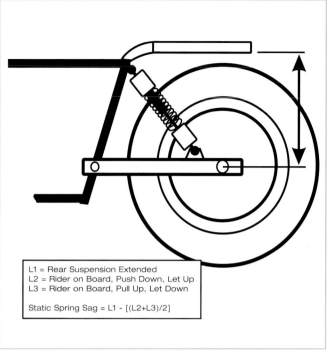

L1 = Rear Suspension Extended
L2 = Rider on Board, Push Down, Let Up
L3 = Rider on Board, Pull Up, Let Down

Static Spring Sag = L1 - [(L2+L3)/2]

When setting up the rear sag, make sure to take the measurements at an angle as close to vertical as possible.

millimeters, or one inch, and let it come back very slowly. Remember, the rider should be aboard. When the suspension stops, measure the distance between the axle and the mark on the chassis that you used previously. If there is no drag, or friction, in the linkage, the bike will come up a little farther than when it was pushed down. It's important that you do not bounce the rear end as this will cause an inaccurate measurement. This measurement is called "L2."

Step 3: Have your assistant lift up the rear of the bike about 25 millimeters, or one inch, and let it down very slowly. Record a measurement where the suspension stops. If there were no drag, or friction, it would drop a little further than the original measurement, or L2. Remember not to bounce the suspension. This measurement is called "L3."

Step 4: The sag is in the middle of L2 and L3. In fact, if there is no drag in the linkage, L2 and L3 will be the same. To get the actual sag number, find the midpoint by averaging the two numbers and subtracting them from the fully extended measurement of L1. Static Spring Sag = L1 - [(L2+L3)/2]

Step 5: Adjust the spring preload using whatever method applies to your bike. Spring collars are common, and some of these need special tools to be adjusted. In a

MEASURING STATIC SPRING SAG

REAR SUSPENSION

Step 1. Suspension Fully Extended L1_____________

Step 2. Rider On-board, Push Down, Let Up L2__________

Step 3. Rider On-board, Lift Up, Let Down L3__________

3-6
embedded file
hold rule

FORMULA for static spring sag

Static Spring Sag = L1 - [(L2+L3)/2]

Static Spring Sag, Rear = __________

REAR SETTINGS

	Travel		% of Total Travel
Off-Road Bikes	95-100mm		30-33%
Off-Road 80cc Mini's	75-80mm		30-33%
Street Bikes	30-35mm		28-33%
Road Race Bikes	25-30mm		23-27%

Rear Suspension Stiction (mechanical condition) = L3 - L2

Stiction __________

Rear Suspension, Good Condition = 3mm (.12")
Rear Suspension, Poor Condition = 10mm (.39")

FRONT SUSPENSION

Step 1. Suspension Fully Extended L1_____________

Step 2. Rider On-board, Push Down, Let Up L2_____________

Step 3. Rider On-board, Lift Up, Let Down L3_____________

FORMULA for static spring sag

Static Spring Sag = L1 - [(L2+L3)/2]

Static Spring Sag, Front = __________

FRONT SETTINGS

	Travel		% of Total Travel
Off-Road Bikes	75-85mm		25-28%
Off-Road 80cc Mini's	65-70mm		25-28%
Street Bikes	30-35mm		28-33%
Road Race Bikes	25-30mm		23-27%

Front Suspension Stiction (mechanical condition) = L3 - L2

Stiction __________

Front Suspension, Good Condition = 15mm (.59")
Front Suspension, Poor Condition = 40mm (1.57")

SPRING RATE TEST (rear end)

This spring rate test measures Free sag, which is the amount the bike settles under its own weight (no rider on board).

REAR SUSPENSION

Off-Road Bikes	15-25mm	
Off-Road 80cc Mini's	10-20mm	
Street Bikes	0-5mm	(should not top-out too hard)
Road Race Bikes	0-5mm	(should not top-out too hard)

When Race sag is correct and the Free sag is LESS than the minumum recommended (if it tops-out for example), a LIGHTER spring is needed.

When the Race sag is correct and the Free sag is MORE than the maximum recommended, a HEAVIER spring is needed

Use this worksheet to determine the best suspension settings for your motorcycle.

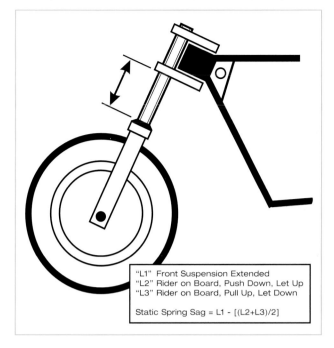

"L1" Front Suspension Extended
"L2" Rider on Board, Push Down, Let Up
"L3" Rider on Board, Pull Up, Let Down

Static Spring Sag = L1 - [(L2+L3)/2]

Measure sag on standard forks as shown. For inverted forks, use the front axle instead of the lower triple clamp as the other measuring point for measuring sag.

pinch, you can use a blunt chisel to unlock the locking collar and turn the main adjusting collar. For road race bikes, rear sag is typically 25 to 30 millimeters. Street riders usually use 30 to 35 millimeters. If you have too much sag, you need more preload; if you have too little sag, you need less preload. The firmer settings commonly used on the track are generally not desirable for street use because they can't compensate for the larger obstacles found on public roads.

If you adjust the preload to its stiffest setting and still have too much sag, you need stiffer springs. If you adjust the preload to its minimum setting and can't get enough sag, you need shorter or lighter springs.

Front Suspension

Front-end sag is measured in a similar manner to rear-end sag. However, it is much more critical to take seal drag into account on the front forks because it is more pronounced and has a greater effect on your measurements.

Step 1: Extend the fork completely and measure from the wiper (the dust seal atop the slider) to the bottom of the triple clamp (or lower fork casting on inverted forks), as shown in figure 2. This measurement is called "L1."

Step 2: Take the bike off the sidestand and put the rider on board in a riding position. Get an assistant to balance the bike from the rear, then push down on the front end and let it extend very slowly. Where the forks slider stops, measure the distance between the wiper and the bottom of the triple clamp again. Do not bounce the front forks. This measurement is called "L2."

Step 3: Lift up on the front end and let it drop very slowly. Where it stops, measure again. Don't bounce the suspension. This measurement is called "L3." Once again, L2 and L3 are different due to stiction or drag in the seals and bushings. Stiction is particularly higher for telescopic front forks than for the rear suspension.

Step 4: Just as with the rear suspension, halfway between L2 and L3 is where the sag would be with no drag or stiction. Therefore, L2 and L3 must be averaged and subtracted from L1 to calculate true sag. Static Spring Sag = L1 - [(L2+L3)/2]

Step 5: To adjust sag, use the preload adjusters, if available, or vary the length of the preload spacers inside the fork. Street bikes should have 25 to 33 percent of their total travel, which equates to 30 to 35 millimeters of sag. Road race bikes usually run 25 to 30 millimeters of sag.

This method of checking sag takes stiction into account and also allows you to check the drag of the linkage and seals. The greater the difference between the measurements L2 and L3, or between the pushing down and pulling up, the worse the stiction. A good low-friction linkage for rear suspension should have less than three millimeters difference. A bad linkage has a more than 10 millimeters difference between L2 and L3. Forks in good condition have less than 15 millimeters difference. Forks with more than 40 millimeters difference between the two measurements need to be carefully inspected and rebuilt.

Using different sag on the front and rear will have a huge effect on handling. More sag on the front or less sag on the rear will make the bike turn quicker. Less sag on the front or more sag on the rear will make the bike turn slower. Increasing sag will also decrease bottoming resistance, though spring rate has a bigger effect than sag in bottoming. Racers often use less sag to keep the bike higher off the ground for more ground clearance. Because road racers work with much heavier braking and steering forces than normally encountered on the street, they use a stiffer setup.

It's important to stress that, when calculating sag, there is no magic or correct answer to the equation. You may like the feel of the bike with less or more sag than described in these guidelines. Your personal sag and front-to-rear sag bias will depend on several factors including type of riding, chassis geometry, track or road conditions, tire selection, and rider weight and preferences.

Suspension Troubleshooting

Forks

1. Suspension Too Soft, Bottoms, Wallows
   - Oil level too low
   - Not enough compression damping
   - Spring rate too soft
   - Not enough spring preload
   - Dirt in valving, broken or bent valve, burr on piston or shim
   - Damping rod bushing worn out
   - Compression valve O-ring broken
   - Damping rod not attached to fork cap

2. Front End Too Stiff—Harsh, Nervous, Twitchy
   - Compression damping adjustment set too high
   - Internal compression damping too high
   - Spring rate too stiff
   - Too much rebound damping
   - Oil level too high
   - See #6

3. Dynamic Ride Height Too Low, Oversteers
   - Spring rate too soft
   - Not enough spring preload
   - Not enough compression damping
   - Rebound too high
   - Anything that makes the rear higher than the front

4. Dynamic Ride Height Too High, Doesn't Turn Well, Understeers, Pushes
   - Too much spring preload
   - Spring rate too high
   - Too much compression damping
   - Rear of bike riding too low
   - Anything that makes the rear higher than the front
   - See #6

5. Dives Under Braking
   Note: All motorcycles do this to some extent. Total dive is controlled by spring forces (rate, preload, and air/oil ratio) only.
   - See #3

6. Sticky Forks
   - Axle clamp not centered—fork tubes misaligned
   - Fork brace broken or out of adjustment
   - Fork seals not broken-in or poor design (aftermarket)
   - Fork seals not lubricated
   - Poor quality fork oil or needs replacing
   - Bent fork tubes, axle, triple clamps (crash damage)
   - Fork sliders dented or pitted
   - Poor fork bushing design (aftermarket)
   - Triple clamp too tight
   - Bushings damaged, dented, or worn out
   - Metal imbedded in fork bushings caused by:
       Preload washers not located properly
       Aluminum preload washers used
       Steel spring spacer contacting aluminum fork cap
       Fork cap threads "shedding" on installation
   - Cartridge rod bushing too tight
   - Spring guide rubbing on I.D. of spring (guide grows from use of solvent when cleaning)
   - Fork spring too large an O.D.

7. Hard to Turn
   - Rear end rides too low
   - Spring rate too stiff
   - Too much preload
   - Too much tire pressure
   - Seat height too low or handlebars too high and/or narrow
   - See #4
   - See #6

8. Front End Feels Loose
   - Not enough rebound damping
   - Damping rod bushings worn out
   - Steering bearings loose or worn
   - Tire pressure too low
   - Chassis flex
   - Worn out rebound piston ring
   - Fork fluid needs changing
   - Fork oil cavitation (foaming)

9. Steering Head Shakes
   - Chassis not straight
   - Misalignment of front and rear wheels
   - Fork flex, chassis flex, or swingarm flex

- Fork oil level too high
- Bottom out mechanism too long
- Too much rebound damping
- Not enough rebound damping
- Too much compression damping
- Poor tire compound or wrong type of tire
- Tire not mounted on rim correctly
- Wheel out of balance
- Brake rotor bent or warped
- Worn out or loose steering head bearings
- Anything that makes the front end lower than the rear
- "Death grip" on bars while riding
- See #6

10. Deflects on Square Edge Bumps
    - Too much compression damping
    - Spring rate too stiff
    - Too much spring preload
    - Too much compression damping
    - See #6

11. Leaky Fork Seals
    - Nicks, pits, or rust on fork tubes
    - Bent fork tubes
    - Worn bushings or seals
    - Improper seal installation

Shocks

1. Rear End Kicks or Skips
   Note: This is the most commonly misdiagnosed symptom. Usually diagnosed as not enough rebound damping, it is usually caused by too much compression damping and/or too stiff a spring.
   - Too much compression damping
   - Spring rate too stiff
   - Too much spring preload
   - Too much rebound damping (*not* too little)
   - Linkage bearings worn, too tight, or no lubrication
   - Tire pressure too high
   - See #3

2. Rear End Tries to Swap w/Front
   - Too much compression damping
   - Not enough rebound damping
   - Spring rate too stiff or too soft
   - Rear shock bottoms out
   - See #3

3. Sticky Rear Shock(s)
   - Linkage not maintained (if applicable)
   - Swingarm bearings not maintained
   - Shock eyelet bearings not lubricated
   - Floating brake rod or backing plate not lubricated
   - Missing or improper bearing spacers
   - Bent shock shaft

4. Rear End Feels Loose
   - Not enough rebound damping
   - Not enough compression damping

5. Poor Traction
   - Too much compression or rebound damping
   - Not enough rebound damping
   - Tire pressure too high
   - Poor tire selection/compound
   - Tires worn out
   - Too much spring preload
   - Spring rate too stiff
   - See #3

6. Not Tracking
   - Too much rebound damping
   - Too much compression damping
   - See #3

7. Rear Bottoms Out
   - Too much static sag
   - Not enough compression damping
   - Spring rate too soft
   - Piston ring or O-ring worn
   - Suspension fluid worn out
   - Shock seal leaking
   - Loss of nitrogen causing oil cavitation (foaming)

Chapter 16
Ergonomics

Most touring riders are well versed in the importance of ergonomics. Their extended hours in the saddle magnify small comfort problems. Unfortunately, many sport riders give the subject too little, if any, thought, even though ergonomics can have a dramatic impact on bike control.

Ergonomics is the study of how man relates to his machine. For a motorcyclist, this comes down to the points where rider and vehicle make contact. Think of these points as the controls. When your controls are correctly sized and positioned, your inputs are more efficient, and your mind is free to concentrate on what is happening, rather than on how uncomfortable you are. Regardless of your skill level, you can only truly ride your best when you are comfortable.

I first became aware of the importance of ergonomics while racing my 125 in club races at Willow Springs. Even after a short practice session, I would come in with severe cramps and pains. I was convinced that the people who engineered these racing "tiddlers" did not have me in mind when they laid out the controls. The pegs were too high and too far forward, the seat was too low, and the fairing was too narrow for my body to fold up behind it.

I began working on each control to try to correct the problems. With some custom hangers, I was able to move the pegs back and down about an inch each. It was certainly in the right direction. I then added a seat pad that was a half-inch thicker than my previous one. To combat the windblast, I fitted slightly wider mounts for both the upper and lower fairings. A call to Zero Gravity (www.zerogravity-racing.com; 800-345-9791) netted me a larger-than-stock windscreen. Together, these seemingly insignificant changes added enough extra comfort that I was not getting cramped at the end of a race, and I was able to lower my lap times by a full second. Although a second a lap may not seem like much to a non-racer, keep in mind that in a 12-lap race, that amounts to 12 seconds. And it's not uncommon for 10 riders or more to be separated by less than 12 seconds at the end of a race.

Comfort

The primary internal factors affecting ergonomic comfort are related to bloodflow, pressure, and skin temperature. When you sting, or when part of you "falls asleep," your body is letting you know that you aren't getting enough bloodflow. Bloodflow is affected by excessive pressure. For instance, when sitting for long periods of time, the ischial tuberosities, the small, bony rails at the base of the pelvis, dig into soft tissue in your gluteus maximus, blocking off small capillaries. As a result, you will start to feel the sting.

Holding any body position requires some degree of muscle tension. Being in one position for too long, or restricting full extension of any muscle group for an extended period of time limits bloodflow. This can easily happen when you are crouched over on a sportbike. The solution is to stretch out, or relax, the affected areas to get the blood pumping again. In a sense, this process can hose away your body's "waste" products.

Cold weather causes your body to reduce bloodflow to your extremities first, to protect its internal organs. That's why your fingers and toes get cold first. Hot temperatures cause your body to cool itself by perspiring. Leaving sweat on the skin surface for too long causes irritation.

Handlebars

Handlebars are an obvious place to start with any ergonomic evaluation because they are the primary component used to position the rider's upper body. Wider bars provide more leverage for steering, which is important when riding larger and heavier bikes. This riding benefit usually comes with the penalty of more wrist radial deviation. In other words, your wrist is cocked with your thumbs closer to your arm. To find the correct width for a given application, you must find a balance between making steering easier on your arms and adding pressure to your wrist bones.

Whether or not you use a windshield may also change your bar preference. The less wind protection and more speed you encounter, the more aerodynamic (leaned forward) you need to be to handle the air pressure pushing you backwards. If you can find a pair of adjustable bars that fit your model, experimentation is a lot easier.

Hand Controls

Grips are one of the most overlooked areas of ergonomics. They probably your most critical connection to the suspension, brakes, and, most importantly, tires, yet many sport riders don't think twice about them. I think every motorcyclist should spend some

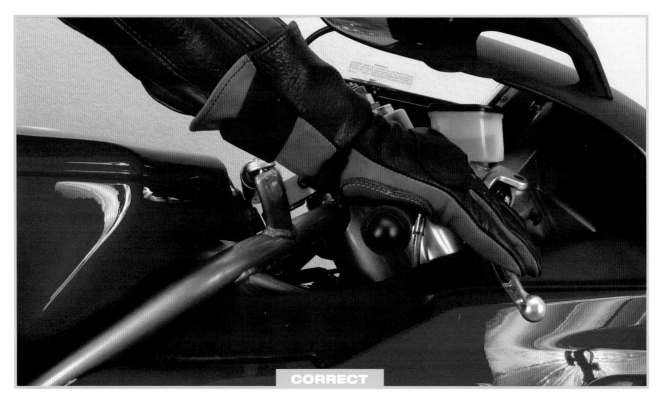

The most common control setup problem is having the clutch and brake levers set too high (top). This causes a wrist extension condition that becomes increasingly painful over time. Placing the wrist in a functionally neutral position (bottom), most efficiently transmits the forces from your upper body. Translation: it takes less muscle effort to steer and resist braking forces, and prevents undue wrist strain, making it more comfortable as well.

Having something for your butt to rest against during hard acceleration keeps your arms from working too hard to keep you from sliding off the back. During a 24-hour endurance race in Spain we used this adjustable padding setup to compensate for the differences in rider height.

Many sportbikes are quite uncomfortable for regular street use but Heli Bars can help make the pain go away without compromising performance. For comparison, this Yamaha R1 is equiped with a Heli Bar on the left side and a stock unit on the right. Heli Bars are taller, farther rearward, and utilize all the stock cables for a simple bolt-on improvement.

Because no control setup will fit all riders or conditions, some bikes like this Ducati 999 have adjustable controls. In this case the footpeg bracket can be located using several different sets of mounting holes, while the brake lever uses a sliding mount. Note that even the swingarm pivot point can be adjusted up and down by using different shaped inserts in the oblong hole.

time experimenting with different widths, thickness, and patterns of grips. As a general guideline, I have found that thinner, harder, and narrower grips offer better feel and control. Conversely, thicker, softer, wider, and more barrel-shaped grips offer more comfort and vibration damping. Every pair of hands is different so find the best fit for you.

Small controls like levers, switches, and even footpegs can have a sizable effect on comfort, too. When Buell wanted to sell motorcycles to Ducati riders,

it kept getting the same complaint from prospective customers. Everyone was saying that the big Harley controls felt awkward. Buell listened and changed the controls for the S1 Lightning to the exact same components used by Ducati. After riding an SI with control changes, I was amazed at how much better the bike felt when compared to the S2.

Seats

Seats are another area of ergonomic importance.

Unless you are using a backrest, many cruiser seats force your lower spine into a bowed-out position that will soon become painful. To fix it requires the seating area to be perpendicular to the ground or even sloping forward to rotate your pelvis counter-clockwise, which will achieve proper lumbar lordosis (curvature of the lower back). That is the position your spine naturally assumes when standing.

And I don't mean just their height. If you make a "butt print" by sitting down in the sand, you will see the concave shape that helps distribute your weight over the largest possible surface area. When it comes to comfort, the shape of the seat is actually much more important than the foam material on top of it. In fact, a properly designed, solid steel tractor seat can be more comfortable than many motorcycle seats. Farmers can drive those things all day without being in pain, and those seats don't have *any* padding. Of course, because bums come in all shapes and sizes, there is no one "perfect" shape.

The reason so many motorcycle seats are uncomfortable is because the manufacturers learned a long time ago that seats shaped for comfort don't feel good in the showroom and vice versa. A small seat that is narrow in front makes it easy to stand up while straddling the bike on the sale floor, but that same seat is exactly what makes for poor long distance comfort on the road. Of course, there are plenty of aftermarket seat makers out there who would love to sell you a replacement.

Feeling

In the automotive world, Mazda has been a real ergonomics pioneer. It was one of the first manufacturers to take a serious look at not only where controls were placed but how they felt in operation. Mazda went as far

As a rule cruiser-type motorcycles tend to be as uncomfortable as racer-replica sportbikes, but Harley-Davidson's Road Glide is an exception. While it might look as stylish as most cruisers, at its core it is really a touring bike, based on Harley's comfortable (and defunct) Tour Glide.

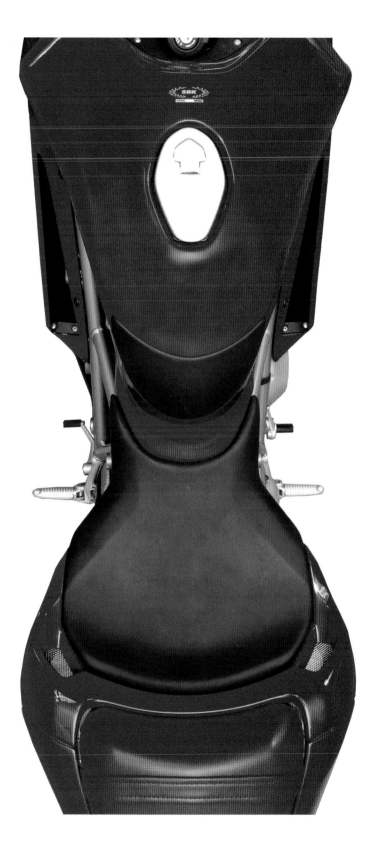

as hooking people to biofeedback machines while they were driving to figure out exactly what types of sensations drivers liked. Anyone who has ever had the pleasure of shifting a five-speed RX-7 or Miata can attest to Mazda's success in this field. Even its old slogan, "It just feels right," emphasizes ergonomic importance.

When Triumph set out to design the T595 Daytona, it obviously had the Ducati 916 in mind as a benchmark. Not only was its styling completely derivative of the Duck, but so was its approach to the control surfaces. Triumph decided the best way to make the bike feel like a Ducati was to use similar components. The grips, bars, switchgear, foot controls, and maybe more came from the same suppliers used by its Bolognese competition. Many components even had the exact same part numbers. Sure enough, the result yielded a surprisingly familiar feel, though no one would ever confuse the Triumph for a Ducati.

Hopefully the manufacturers will take a more "feeling" approach to motorcycle design in the future so bikes will not only work better, but feel better, too. After all, part of the joy of riding is how it makes you feel.

A wide, concave-shaped seat distributes pressure evenly across the surface area of your butt. A narrow gas tank not only allows your legs to be in a more comfortable position, but it also gives your body more leverage to transition the bike from side to side. As an added bonus, a narrow tank allows your legs to be held closer in, reducing frontal area and the resulting aerodynamic drag. With all these important benefits, it's amazing more manufacturers don't follow Ducati's example in this area.

Chapter 17
Aerodynamics

When it comes to going fast on motorcycles, most of the technical talk centers on engines and suspension systems. But there is an equally important factor that is almost an afterthought: aerodynamics.

Aerodynamics is a branch of a larger engineering discipline called fluid mechanics. It concentrates on how objects, like airplanes and motorcycles, move through the air. The purpose of fluid mechanics is to design vehicles that travel faster and more efficiently. The engineers achieve this by creating shapes that require less force to displace a given volume of air as they move through it.

In Formula One car racing, effective aerodynamics is so prized aerodynamicists are the highest paid engineers on the team. In fact, the top experts command seven-figure salaries! This is because even small improvements in aerodynamics are equivalent to huge increases in horsepower.

Today's motorcycle designs are starting to take aerodynamics more seriously in an attempt to enhance both performance and rider comfort. Ultimately, however, marketers generally determine the shapes of motorcycle bodywork based on by looks rather than engineers

determining the shapes for performance gains. This is because a motorcycle has to look cool to sell well. The truth is that a truly aerodynamic motorcycle like the Buell RW750 looks more like a bland Boeing 737 than a sexy Ducati 916. There have been a few exceptions like John Britten's namesake V1000 so at least there's hope other manufacturers can build more bikes that offer both superior looks and performance.

Pressure vs. Velocity

Before you can discuss what constitutes an aerodynamic shape, you must understand how airflow works. Airflow utilizes the concepts of pressure and velocity, which are inversely proportional to one another. As a bike displaces the air that it moves through, that air must get around the bike in the same way water flows around a rock in the middle of a stream. For example, air that hits in the middle of the fairing builds up pressure until it can make its way around the outside of the fairing. This is why ram air systems pull their charge from the leading edge of the fairing. It's like getting extra air for free because it's under pressure. Just like a pressurized scuba tank can hold a lot of air in a little bit of space.

Because the air making its way around the motorcycle has a longer distance to travel than the surrounding air, it must accelerate to keep up. This acceleration causes the pressure to drop, creating a vacuum effect. Anywhere pressure builds up, there will automatically be a lower-pressure area opposite it. This behavior can be likened to having a vacuum cleaner acting in the low pressure area pulling it backwards. Aircraft use this principle to fly. By shaping the wings with a longer curve on top than underneath, the air on top of the wing must accelerate to cover the longer distance and meet up with the air on the other side. This creates low pressure on top of the wing which, in turn, causes lift. As a result, the planes are "sucked" into the sky.

On a motorcycle, the low-pressure area is generally behind it. In this case, the term "aerodynamic drag" makes sense because the vacuum causes the bike to feel like it's dragging something behind it, limiting its acceleration and top speed.

Aerodynamic drag is measured in numeric form as a coefficient of drag, or Cd, and must be measured in a wind tunnel. Unfortunately, aerodynamic drag does not increase in a linear fashion. It increases exponentially. For example, a Yamaha TZ750 racer requires 21 horsepower to achieve 100 miles per hour. To hit 200 miles per hour, it would need 168 horsepower. And 300 miles per hour would require 567 horsepower! As you can see, a slight aerodynamic improvement can equal a lot of horsepower.

Reducing Aerodynamic Drag

Water forms the shape of a teardrop when taking the path of least resistance through the air. Generally speaking, this is what an aerodynamic vehicle must resemble to minimize aerodynamic drag. Because two-wheelers lean into turns, there are also stability issues that go beyond the aerodynamic shape. This is the main reason we no longer see the "dustbin" fairings that dominated racing in the 1950s. For the purpose of this chapter, however, I will concentrate on the basics of aerodynamic drag.

One of the most important factors relating to aerodynamic drag on a motorcycle is frontal area. Frontal area is simply the surface area facing the direction of movement as viewed from the front of the vehicle. To compare the frontal area of two vehicles, simply take frontal pictures of each one from exactly the same location. To mean something in the real world, include a rider in the measurements. It's important to use the same rider in actual riding gear on both bikes in a standard racer's tuck. Next, lay a piece of graph paper over each photograph and draw an outline around the bike. By calculating how many squares (including partial squares) are contained within the outline, you can come up with a rough approximation of how the models compare in terms of relative frontal area. When it comes to frontal area, less is better.

If frontal area were the only thing guiding aerodynamics, the smallest fairings would be the best choice for every motorcycle. However, the actual shape of the bodywork is more important than the frontal area in determining how much aerodynamic drag the bike will produce.

As mentioned earlier, the ideal body shape resembles a teardrop. Its widest section should be one third of the way back on the bike and should be the same width as the widest part of the rider's shoulders. Its tail should start at the widest part of the rider's hips and converge at no more than a 14-degree included angle. Based on wind tunnel research, 7 degrees per side is the maximum angle you can close an airstream without causing separation. As soon as the air separates, it becomes turbulent and causes drag. It should be noted that, in talking with many Bonneville top-speed racers, an 8-degree included angle, or an angle of 4 degrees per

One of the most aerodynamic motorcycles of the modern era, the 1983 Buell RW750 two-stroke used a fairing based on Harley-Davidson's groundbreaking wind tunnel research of 1969. This is one of the few road racers with a fairing as wide as the rider's shoulders and a seat as wide as the rider's butt.

side, is said to be a more realistic number given the myriad factors encountered in real world conditions.

Unfortunately, if a bike followed these ideal parameters, it would be much too long to be practical and would have a sharp and dangerous tail section. The best way around this dilemma is to imagine the correct shape and then cut off the back of the tail at the back of the rear tire. This is known as a Kamm tail, named after the man who first thought of it. The Kamm tail tricks the air into acting almost like the tail was still there. Bell used a

similar design on a racing helmet that Eddie Lawson used to win the Daytona 200.

Effective motorcycle design also uses the rider's body as an active part in the bike's aerodynamics, filling in the space between the fairing and the tail section. Erik Buell's original 1983 RW750 two-stroke road racer used this principle and is still considered one of the most aerodynamic racing motorcycles ever built.

In 1996, as part of a magazine article examining the aerodynamic effectiveness of sportbikes, I commis-

Beginning track riders often lose precious mph by not keeping their heads down and out of the airstream.

sioned Jim Reed and Charlie Moore to see what kind of top speed improvements we could make without a wind tunnel by simply applying the principles discussed here. The results were astounding. With three simple aerodynamic enhancements, we increased the top speed of a 1992 Honda CBR600F2 by over 11.3 miles per hour. First, we cut the gas tank down a little to help flatten the rider's back. Second, we removed the entire lower fairing. And finally, we created a tail section similar to the one used on the Buell RW750. To help put this in perspective, the equivalent speed increase would have required over 20 additional horsepower. I can only imagine what we could have accomplished if we had the time and money to create a proper fairing back then.

Cooling Drag

One of the biggest aerodynamic problems current sportbikes have is making room for the huge radiators required to keep them cool. More specifically, the problem is the placement of the radiators. By putting them behind the front wheel, much of the cooling air gets blocked, necessitating huge surface areas to compensate for the lack of flow. The increase in aerodynamic drag caused by the engine's cooling system is called cooling drag.

Open-wheel and prototype race cars use seemingly tiny radiators to effectively deal with much higher heat loads than bikes do because they're positioned to optimize airflow. A much better position for the radiator on a motorcycle is under the seat, so long as air can be ducted to it. A few prototype race bikes, like the Britten, have successfully used this type of a system with a relatively small radiator. A primary benefit of this setup is a considerably smaller frontal area.

Unfortunately, with the exception of the new $35,000 Benelli Tornado, most mainstream manufacturers haven't embraced this technology yet, Interestingly, Harley-Davidson developed a trick under-seat radiator setup for its ill-fated Nova project in the 1970s, but it never saw production.

In order to reduce the cooling drag on a traditional radiator setup, internal ducts are needed. This is because drag is created when the air that goes through the radiator finds its way around the engine and eventually gets past the bike. The idea is to

The use of aerodynamic humps on leathers is de rigueur these days. They help fill in some of the low-pressure area behind the rider's helmet and smooth the shape of the rider's back. While they won't add much, if any, top speed to a bike, they do minimize the amount of drag on the helmet, which can significantly reduce neck fatigue. In fact, the moment a special prototype hump I designed ripped off its temporary Velcro attachment at 160 mph, it felt like 10 pounds had been added to my head!

capture as much air as possible from behind the radiator and direct it in as straight a path as possible back into the airstream.

Erik Buell recommends running the internal ducting into a reverse NACA duct as far back on the fairing as possible. The 7-degree rule applies here, as well, so you want to make sure the final duct releases the hot air out of the fairing at no more than a 7-degree angle. The good news is that the high-speed, low-pressure air going around the outside of the fairing will actually help suck the hot air out of the radiator, dramatically increasing its efficiency. If you can somehow seal the system, its efficiency will increase greatly

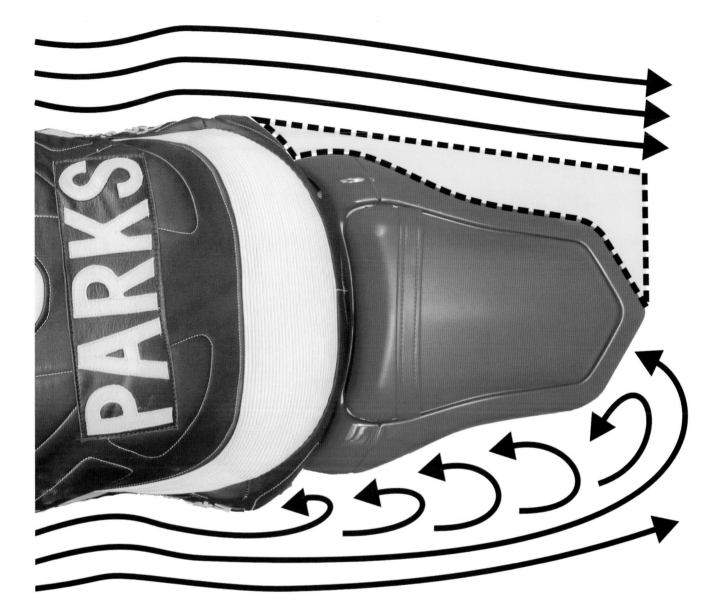

It's virtually impossible to find a modern sportbike with an aerodynamic tail section. Shown from above is a 2003 Ducati 999 with rider aboard. As you can see on the rider's left side, it is too narrow to keep the airflow attached, forming drag-inducing, turbulent "eddies." The flat back, Kamm-style fix, as proposed on the opposite side in yellow, follows the "7-degree rule" of converging at no more than 7 degrees per side to keep the air attached for minimum drag. This type of improvement made on both sides should provide a 2-5 mph increase in top speed. The under-seat exhaust also helps fill in the low-pressure area behind the bike.

Believe it or not, some WWII fighter planes had such aerodynamically efficient cooling systems that the cold air flowing through the hot radiators actually developed thrust! Although I don't think a motorcycle cooling system can be that efficient, I would estimate that you could reduce cooling drag by up to 80 percent by following the suggestions above.

Rider Drag

I realize many of you do not have the time or wherewithal to make some of these radical modifications to your bike, but the goal of these lessons is to teach the importance of aerodynamic drag on performance and examine how your body position contributes to it. One of the best things you

The radical $35,000 Benelli Tornado minimizes cooling drag by positioning the radiator under the seat and ducting fresh air to it. When the bike is not moving, two fans under the taillight help keep things cool by creating a vacuum to suck air through the radiator.

Comparing the frontal areas on different bikes is easy. Simply take a picture of them from the front with an outfitted rider on board (from the exact same height and distance), and lay graph paper on the photo. By counting the number of squares (including partial ones) that are covered by bike or rider, you can make an accurate comparison. While you can see Ducati did a pretty good job of keeping the rider out of the airstream on the 999, there is still room for improvement. The upper fairing should be wider and taller to cover the rider's knee pucks, hands, and shoulders. Also, the rear brake pedal should be farther inboard because it forces the rider's toe into the airstream. A taller windscreen would also help reduce neck fatigue without adding to the frontal area.

Tucking in behind the fairing is not a comfortable position to be in, but it makes a real difference in straight-line performance.

can do to improve the straight line performance of your bike is to practice getting your body out of the airflow. In fact, many beginning track riders lose as much as 7 or 8 miles per hour of top speed on the straights because they are not getting their heads down correctly.

The easiest way to gauge the effectiveness of your body position is to stand your bike vertically in front of a mirror and get on it wearing all your normal riding gear. Next, crouch down, look at where your body is sticking out beyond the fairing (if it has one), and figure out how much you can minimize the protrusions. This is also a good time to think about what modifications you could make to cover up more of your exposed parts. A larger windscreen could be one

helpful addition. Of course, you might also see the benefits of a diet at this point.

Comfort is another consideration when looking at your bike's aerodynamics. If the wind blast from that oddly shaped fairing is rattling your head around, or the low-pressure area caused by that barn-door windshield feels like it's sucking your helmet off your head, you now have enough basic understanding of the forces at work to make some meaningful hypotheses about how to fix them. Sometimes, even in a racing situation, a change that improves rider comfort can be worthwhile even if it slightly reduces aerodynamic efficiency. This is because the net result will be significantly less fatigue, and this can really improve your ability to control the motorcycle.

Aerodynamic efficiency plays a much larger role on the racetrack than it does on the street, but even on a streetbike having at least a small fairing to smooth the airflow makes riding more comfortable.

Chapter 18
Chassis Tuning

There is more to handling than just suspension setup. Chassis geometry also plays an important roll. As discussed in chapter 2, motorcycle chassis' are designed for specific handling characteristics through the use of steering head angle, trail, and even swingarm slope. Because your idea of the ideal handling characteristics for your bike may be different from the ideas of the engineers who designed it, tailoring these specifications can make a dramatic improvement in how your bike handles. Small changes can make a big difference so don't make too big of a change at any one time.

Generally speaking, when the front end of a motorcycle is lowered or its rear is raised, the bike will steer quicker, and less effort will be required on the bars. Of course, the trade-off is less stability. Therefore, anytime the rear is lowered and the front is raised, stability will improve at the expense of steering quickness. There is no perfect setup for any particular bike as it really depends on how each rider likes his bike to behave.

Touring and cruising riders generally prefer more stability, and sport riders like to be able to change direction quickly without having to put a ton of effort on the bars. Still, many tourers and cruisers can benefit from quicker steering than stock, and some sportbikes like the 1993-1997 CBR900RRs, can benefit from slowing down

G.M.D. Computrack's Kent Soignier measures an SV650 street bike to see if it has any chassis misalignments. In addition to fixing crash damage, the company's chassis optimization services can improve the handling of any bike. Think of it as a motorcycle chiropractor.

the steering because they steer too quickly as delivered and can feel "nervous." Because these adjustments must make the chassis achieve a balance between quickness and stability, it's best to experiment in little steps to see which compromises are right for you.

A common misconception is that spring preload adjustments should be used to change ride height. Although they do affect ride height, the purpose of spring preload adjustments is to raise or lower the point at which the bike rides on its suspension. Correct spring preload will take the rider's weight into account and set the suspension so as to minimize bottoming and topping out during suspension travel.

Making Changes

There are several methods for changing ride height independently of spring preload. Raising the position of the front fork tubes in the triple clamp effectively lowers the front end. A somewhat similar effect can be accomplished by raising the rear of the bike. This

Adjusting a motorcycle's rear ride height can make big improvements to its handling. While most motorcycles don't come with this feature, some stock shocks can be updated with an adjuster like this GSX-R unit from Engineered Racing Products.

usually requires the use of an aftermarket shock as most stock rear shocks, even on sportbikes, don't have ride height adjusters.

I have often heard riders swear that after changing their brand of tires, their bikes handled differently. Some believed their bikes handled better, and others were convinced their bikes handled worse. In reality, this is often the result of different front-to-rear tire circumferences and not necessarily the tires themselves. For example, although your bike may be fitted with a 120/70-17 front and 170/60-17 rear tire, the actual measured circumferences of the front and rear tires can be quite different from brand to brand. This is very important to consider when replacing worn out tires. (The circumference of the front tire will also change the calibration of your speedometer, which has led many unsuspecting brand-swapping riders straight to traffic court.)

If the new tires you selected have different circumferences from the originals, your motorcycle's ride height can be significantly changed. If both new tires have the same relative diameters as the old ones, the handling will be closer to the original, with the difference being the inherent tire characteristics. The only way to really know a specific tire's circumference is to measure it, preferably with a clothing tape measure.

In addition to changing tire brands and, as a result, tire circumferences, changing the size of tire, specifically the aspect ratio, can also affect ride height. For example, mounting a 120/60 tire on the front instead of a 120/70 will lower the front of the bike, reducing the rake and trail, and quickening the steering. Remember, don't make too radical of a change to your bike's geometry. It's best to make very small changes so you can see if you're headed in the right direction before going overboard.

Checking Alignment

Chassis alignment that matches a manufacturer's specifications is rare even on a brand new motorcycle. Production tolerances for frame welding, jigs, and materials all play a part in how "off" the end result is. In fact, in some cases, small deviations from the blueprint can add up, or "stack," during the manufacturing process. Consequently, your new bike will be so off that it will exhibit various negative handling quirks.

Frame alignment on a used bike is even more questionable. The bike may be fine, or it may have been crashed and properly repaired, but it also may have been crashed hard (or merely dropped in a parking lot) and been repaired poorly. Something as simple as using too much force when tying a bike down for transport can also bend the chassis. If you've had an accident where the bike hit pavement, chances are the frame is tweaked. Unfortunately, most dealers can't check to see if the chassis is out-of-whack before they start bolting on cosmetic parts, leaving you with a motorcycle that could put your life at risk. Unless a frame is really tweaked, your naked eye won't be able to tell that anything is wrong with it.

The lateral alignment is the only aspect of chassis geometry that is relatively easy to check. Lateral misalignment is when the rear and front tire don't "track" in the same line and are, in fact, offset from one another. If the offset is large enough, it can cause the bike to become unstable even when it is going straight. If this is the case, you will constantly have to push on the right or left side of the handlebars to keep the bike traveling in a straight line.

It should be noted that some manufactures purposely design frames that have the front and rear wheels offset from one another, like the BMW K1200RS and many pre-1999 Harley-Davidsons. This makes lateral alignment on these bikes a moot point.

To check for lateral misalignment, lay face down on the ground in front of the front wheel with your arms outstretched in front of you. Line up your left eye with the left edge of the rear tire. Then, mark the corresponding spot to the left of the front tire on the ground with your left index finger. Without moving your left hand, reposition your head so your right eye aligns with the right edge of the rear tire. Mark that spot with your right hand. When the front wheel is straight, the distance between those two points should be equal. The average person can see a 5–8mm offset using this method.

Of course, for the measurement to be accurate you must first make sure the rear wheel is aligned to the swingarm pivot, or you may just be pointing the rear wheel straight at an out-of-alignment front wheel. If you're looking for a tool for that job, I'm especially fond of the Rohm Performance Machine (530-674-9123) Line Right. Although a little pricey at $89.95, it should provide

years of service. For around $150, you could also get your bike professionally measured at a G.M.D. Computrack center.

G.M.D. Computrack

I don't want to sound like a commercial, but currently there is only one company that has the means to accurately check every aspect of your bike's chassis alignment. G.M.D. Computrack (www.gmdcomputrack.com) has been in business for almost 20 years. It has centers all over the United States and is constantly perfecting its system of chassis measurement and optimization. G.M.D. Computrack uses a sophisticated three-axis optical coordinate system to make incredibly precise and repeatable measurements, and has specialized equipment to straighten a chassis back to "normal." G.M.D. Computrack's business is an even mix of crash repair and race bike optimization.

The most impressive part of the G.M.D. Computrack system is the company's proprietary "what if" software. Once G.M.D. Computrack has measured your bike, it can tell you how a particular change, like a new tire, will affect all the bike's geometry measurements. Combined with a huge database of what it calls its "sweet numbers," basically chassis setups that work well for a particular motorcycle, you can get a bike setup just how you like it in very short order.

After noticing my Suzuki SV650 race bike couldn't turn as quickly as the bikes of some of my competitors, I decided to get a full G.M.D. Computrack chassis optimization. The results speak for themselves. Not only did I lose a full second a lap but my confidence also improved dramatically, and I never crashed in a race all year. In fact, I won a WERA National Endurance Championship! Of course, you don't have to be a racer to benefit from a tuned chassis. Better handling and improved confidence is important to everyone. If you suspect your bike is out of alignment, or would just like to improve its handling, I highly recommend giving G.M.D. Computrack a call at (866) 332-2244.

Chapter 19
Fitness

Having raced motorcycles since I was 14 years old, the riding benefits of physical fitness have always seemed obvious. But most street riders, and even many club racers, don't take fitness seriously and have no idea how much it can improve their riding.

When you are physically fit, you can ride longer and farther without fatigue. You can respond more effectively to dangers on the road. Plus, you can ride more safely and increase the amount of enjoyment you get out of riding. What motorcyclist would not sacrifice a little sweat in exchange for these benefits?

If you've never raced, you'd probably be surprised by the strength and endurance needed to wrestle modern road and off-road bikes around racetracks. In fact, motorcycle racers are among the fittest athletes in any sport. Because racing is just riding at a higher level, what's good in terms of fitness for the racer is, therefore, good for the street rider.

One of the top experts in the racing fitness field is former motocross champion Gary Semics, a highly-regarded trainer of today's motocross riders. With a client list that includes Ezra Lusk, Jeremy McGrath, Kevin Windam, John Dowd, and Stephane Roncada, Semics knows whereof he speaks. His insights and training tips were essential in creating this guide to high-performance riding fitness.

Riders vs. Racers

One of the toughest physical impacts motorcycle racers, especially those who race off-road, have to contend with is "arm pump." This is an incredibly painful buildup of lactic acid that saps forearm strength, wrist control, and grip strength. And in a Supercross event, for example, these things are vital. To help avoid arm pump, cardiovascular and weight workouts are used to complement a rigorous schedule of practice racing.

Fortunately, most pleasure riders need only pursue a minimum regimen of general conditioning to see significant benefits on the road. By this I mean three days a week of cardiovascular workouts and two days a week of weightlifting.

Cardiovascular Workouts

Pro trainers regard a good cardiovascular workout as one that will raise the heartbeat above normal for a minimum of 20 minutes. This means sustaining your heartbeat at a rate approximately equal to the outcome of the number 200 minus your age. In other words, it means getting your butt off the Barcalounger, getting the blood pumping, and breaking a healthy sweat.

Jogging is great for cardiovascular workouts because supporting your own weight also helps build bone mass. If your knees don't like the impact of running, powerwalking can provide similar benefits as long as the distance is the same.

If you are completely out of shape, you should work up to the 20-minute level in steps. However, if you are in reasonable shape, you can probably start at the 20-minute level and then build your schedule to four or five days per week, keeping your heartbeat up for 20 to 60 minutes at a time depending on how much endurance you want to develop.

You can raise your heartbeat by swimming, bicycling, or running. Stationary bicycles are great for rainy day workouts—assuming you would rather train at home. You should vary your cardiovascular training because each exercise offers different fitness benefits. Plus, varying workouts can also help reduce the risk of repetitive stress injuries.

Stretching before any physical activity—even regular street riding—can greatly reduce cramps and stiffness. The looser your muscles are, the more comfortable you'll feel on a bike.

Weightlifting

If you're a street rider, weightlifting can benefit you as well. Lifting light weights two or three days a week won't turn you into Schwarzenegger, but it will tone your muscles, ligaments, and tendons. Basic weightlifting will also help you maintain a full range of motion and boost blood circulation to your bones and tissues.

To avoid injury, those new to weightlifting should gradually increase the length of their workouts rather than indulge in a weekend warrior blitzkrieg. One set of 15 reps with light weights is a good start. By light weights, I mean whatever feels light for you—all the muscles need is a bit more resistance than they normally get. If you use too much weight, you'll injure the muscles and delay their strengthening—so err on the side of lightness. If the workout provokes no soreness, increase to two sets per workout, then to three. Three sets should be sufficient for good muscle tone. If you add more weight, more reps or more sets, the exercises will start to add bulk. This might be good for winning bar fights, but bulky muscles do nothing to improve your riding.

A proper set should include the following weight exercises: calf raises to build up the area from foot to knee; knee-squats to build up the quads, hamstrings, and gluteus maximus; leg extensions and leg curls, again for the legs; sit-ups and crunches for abdominal muscles; bench presses for chest muscles; seated cable rowing and lateral pull-downs (to the chest rather than behind the head); military press for shoulder muscles; tricep cable press-down for the triceps; arm curls for the biceps; and wrist curls for hands, wrists, and forearms.

Strong and fully functional hands, wrists, and arms are obviously crucial to riding well. I've been in 6- and 24-hour endurance road races where my forearms became so pumped up that they stayed in that painful condition for days afterward. While you don't normally think of riding gear as a factor when it come to arm pump, jackets, leathers, and gloves need to have enough room (or stretch) in them not to constrict the rider under severe conditions.

Arm pump is such a concern to racers that Semics has produced and marketed a training video aimed at eliminating the condition. Call (800) 500-3938 and Gary will gladly sell you his hard-earned knowledge on the subject for $23.95 including shipping. You will probably find Semics' video a worthwhile investment, especially if you're one of those street riders or racers who often ends up with a death grip on the bars when things get moving fast.

Weight machines and free weights will both work adequately for the described regimen, but you should be aware of the distinct advantages each has to offer. For example, free weights not only work your muscles, they require you to exercise your tendons, ligaments, and joints in order to balance the weights as you move them. Weight machines are a lot faster and easier to use. I'm a fan of weight machines because I'll use practically any excuse to get exercising out of the way as quickly as possible.

Remember, if you have any specific physical or health problems, you should see a physician and a physical therapist before starting any weight training. A physical therapist can often analyze problems and design workouts that avoid making them worse.

Motorcycle-Specific Fitness

The more top professionals I speak with these days, the more I hear about the importance of lower back and leg strength. For example, multi-time AMA 250 GP Champion Rich Oliver says that the most important object of training is to strengthen the lower back so that it supports the upper body and arms. This will minimize the load on the arms and hands. Oliver recommends that riders use their hands as tools to control the bike, rather than as a means of support.

Doing back extensions and sit-ups or crunches is an effective way to strengthen the lower back as well as tighten the abdominal muscles that contribute to a strong torso. Oliver says riders also need to have a grip strong enough to avoid the fatigue that comes from throttling, clutching, steering, and braking for extended periods of time.

Back in the late 1980s, I raced a two-stroke Yamaha RZ500 that had four separate carburetors and return springs. The bike required so much force to turn the throttle that my wrists ached for days after a race until I started doing mini-weightlifting exercises to strengthen them. Squeezing a kitchen sponge repetitively is good for combating this type of hand fatigue. A sponge provides just a little bit of resistance, but that's all that's needed. The way Oliver puts it, "Building a lot of forearm and grip strength is not the objective. Endurance is what you're seeking."

The legs also perform an important function in riding, working with the lower back to keep stresses away from the upper body. AMA Superbike Champion Nicky Hayden actually spends an hour a day squeezing the gas tank on his Honda CBR600F4i with his legs in order to build up his thigh muscles. When riding, he uses these muscles to help steer the bike once leaned into a turn.

Good eyesight is also vital for street riders. I had been riding in road and motocross races for years before I had my eyes checked. After straining to read the scoreboard at a basketball game, I finally realized my vision might need some improvement and went in for an eye exam. After being fitted with glasses for the first time in my life, I was shocked to see how much I had been missing. My very next race I dropped 1.5 seconds a lap. For the first time in many years, I could actually see where I was going! This not only made me faster, I felt considerably safer and more confident as well. If you suspect your vision may be less than 20/20, get a checkup. It may be the best single improvement you can make to your riding.

Oliver suspects that a lot of motorcyclists on the street cannot see well enough to be safe and effective riders. Oliver himself has had corrective surgery to make sure his vision is optimal for competition. "The better your vision is," he says, "the quicker your response to situations." Remember that your eyes don't always work

One of the best ways to reduce arm and hand fatigue is by strengthening your lower back so it can support some of your weight. Crunches and back extensions can work wonders on your lower back.

at optimum levels. If you are tired, they can't focus as well, and this can hurt your ability to control the bike.

The conditions of your eyeglasses and your windshield are just as important as your eyesight. If they are dirty or scratched, your vision will be hampered in the same way your reflexes are impaired by alcohol. You should clean optical surfaces with a good microfiber cloth that won't scratch them. If they are already scratched, replace them.

Peripheral vision is also very important. And as a way to train this faculty, Oliver visits the batting cage regularly to develop and maintain quickness of focus, quick reactions, and hand-eye coordination. But, he says, motorcyclists can use other sports, like tennis, which also requires good hand-eye coordination, to get their vision and reflexes in shape. Professional athletes will even employ experts on sports vision who can offer training tips for improving their vision.

Diet

The final part of the fitness equation is diet. You don't have to be fanatical about it, just use common sense and moderation. You want to eat to ride, not ride to eat. Of course, there's nothing wrong with riding to a restaurant to have a sensible meal. Regardless of where you eat, you should remember that reducing the total quantity of food will help keep you from cramping and putting on extra weight. If you feel overstuffed and

Good vision requires keeping your faceshield, windshield, and glasses clean. This is best performed with a good microfiber cloth like this one available for sale at leeparksdesign.com. It is the only material that won't scratch fragile optical plastic.

bloated after a meal, you ate too much.

When reducing quantities, it's important that you not cut out too much protein because it is what helps keep your muscles strong and working properly. Cutting down on excess carbohydrates, like those found in sugars, breads, and pastas, is a good way to save some calories. Remember, the carbohydrates your body doesn't burn eventually get stored as fat.

Preventing Overheating and Dehydration

Keeping cool and hydrated on a motorcycle should be a concern for every motorcyclist, especially when riding hard. Unfortunately, there is a lot of misinformation on the subject, and the strategies for keeping you comfortable will vary depending on climate.

While competing in a six-hour endurance race at Summit Point in 2001, I began to suffer from heat exhaustion, which I was lucky enough to diagnose before it turned into heat stroke. Fortunately, the night before the race I was watching a story on the evening news about a football player who had just died on the field from heat stroke. I had paid enough attention to remember some of the symptoms, which include headache, dizziness, nausea, and tiredness. I had experienced all of them while on the track. As soon as I started feeling incoherent, which is the signal of the onset of heat stroke, I came in immediately.

Frankly, I was shocked by how fast my condition deteriorated. Within only six laps, the 90 percent humidity of West Virginia had done me in. In fact, I had to be carried to our air-conditioned RV where I spent the next four hours curled up in the fetal position. My teammates were smart enough to keep me drinking water. I drank over a gallon before I even had to urinate—that's how dehydrated I was. The scary part is that I thought I had been drinking plenty of fluids throughout the day. Obviously it wasn't enough. The need for hydration in endurance racing is so important that many racers who take part in the Suzuka 8-hour event actually get hooked up to an intravenous drip between stints! Intravenous drips being impractical for high-performance street riding, so you might want to consider using a backpack-style beverage container such as the ones produced by Camelbak. Whichever your solution, it's important to understand heat exhaustion and dehydration in case you or a riding buddy ever show any symptoms.

Evaporative Cooling

Perspiration is the way your body transfers excess heat to the air. This process is called evaporative cooling. Those of us who live in dry climates are fortunate because we can use this process to keep cool in the hottest of temperatures. I once stayed comfortable while riding through the California desert in 130-degree-Fahrenheit temperatures by keeping my long-sleeve cotton shirt drenched in water, zipping an Aerostich jacket over it, and leaving the jacket vents barely open. As long as I kept moving, the little bit of incoming airflow was able to evaporate the water, reducing temperatures by 30 degrees or more!

Another consideration when dealing with hot moving air is your body's "operating temperature" of 98.6 degrees Fahrenheit. Once the ambient temperature rises above this, exposing yourself to the air will heat you up, not cool you down. This is the reason firefighters wear those thick jackets. They need to insulate themselves from the heat of the fire. If ventilation was the answer, they would all be wearing mesh jackets. Ventilation does work well from 80-95 degrees Fahrenheit, but can be counterproductive outside of that range. Because your body uses its water supply to keep itself cool by perspiring, you need to keep it replenished with water or sport drinks.

Sport Drinks

Most of the sport drinks on the market are loaded with huge amounts of sugar and salt. If you really like drinks like Gatorade, it's a good idea to mix them with water, adding one part water for each part sport drink. I prefer nutrient-enhanced water like Glaceau's Smartwater, which contains no sugar. If you're really serious and don't mind spending a little cash, Gary Semics is partial to energy drinks from Cytomax because they're loaded with vitamins and minerals designed to go through the stomach and into your system quickly.

Putting It All Together

Now your mission is clear. By getting yourself in good shape, strengthening your back and legs, building some endurance in your grip, working on your vision and reactions, eating right, and watching your hydration levels, you can experience longer, safer, and more enjoyable rides for a moderate expenditure of time and effort. A happy by-product is that you will probably live a longer and healthier life because your heart will be less likely to give out early, and you will be better able to avoid the accidents that those riders impaired by fatigue, slow reflexes, and sub-par vision may not.

Don't forget to incorporate exercise into your routine. If you're the type of person who enjoys a health club atmosphere, you're already halfway there. If you're like me, however, and find going to health clubs about as much fun as digging ditches, I have another suggestion. Finding a good workout partner can mean the difference between really doing it and blowing it off. Recently, I started helping my buddy Ray by taking his dog Macy an occasional walk. Much to my surprise, I found the experience both fun and invigorating. Now we are up to six miles a day if on foot and 12 miles a day if I take the inline skates. And it doesn't matter what time of day or night I'm interested in working out, Macy is always up for the adventure. On top of that, she has an infectious enthusiasm and pushes us both to keep improving the pace and distance. With a workout partner like that, you can't help but get in great shape.

Yamaha's Rich Oliver says that having excellent vision is critical for going fast on a track and reducing risks on the street. With several national championships to his credit, he ought to know.

Chapter 20
Riding Gear

About 2500 years ago, the Taoist sage Chuang Tze described the ideal relationship between rider and gear. He said, "When the shoe fits, the foot is forgotten." Similarly, when riding gear fits, the body is forgotten. This is an important point because improperly fitting riding gear is not only distracting and uncomfortable, but it also may bind your movements. Either scenario could actually cause a crash, which is the last thing your riding gear should be doing.

Riding gear is designed to keep you comfortable on the road and to protect you from the weather or the ground, should you go down. Indeed, properly chosen and fitted gear can make the difference between a joyous and disastrous ride. All motorcycle apparel represents a compromise between comfort and protection. It's generally easy to achieve either one, but excelling at both is a true art form. Where the best gear falls on the comfort/protection continuum depends on what is most important to you. Making an educated decision on riding gear requires an understanding of quality, materials, and construction.

Although certain riding gear manufacturers have better quality products than others, you can't judge gear based solely on brand. This is because there is virtually always a quality range within any given brand. There are several areas of importance regarding quality.

Country of Origin

Where a product is made can say a lot about what you can expect from it, but there are no hard and fast rules. Ultimately, the quality of a product comes down to meeting price goals which are determined by labor, material, and distribution costs. Industrialized nations with strong economies, like the United States, Germany, and England, can produce first-class products, but they have very high labor costs. This is why many companies produce products overseas. Countries with weaker economies and a cheaper labor force, like Korea, Pakistan, and China, can produce labor-intensive products like jackets, boots, and gloves for much less than the developing nations can. When it comes to simple apparel items like T-shirts, where the majority of the cost is in the material, any country can be competitive.

Because most riding gear is very technical, or labor intensive, the vast majority of it is produced in the Far East. For example, most Harley-Davidson gear is made in Pakistan, and the bulk of Joe Rocket apparel comes from Korea.

Economics

The majority of motorcycle products sold in the industry must travel from distributors to retailers before they reach you. This is one of the main reasons why riding gear is so expensive.

Let's take a pair of boots as an example. The actual cost of manufacturing the boots is about $24. To make money, the "manufacturer," who, in many, cases should more accurately be called an importer, raises price to around $34. The warehouse distributor will mark the price up to around $53. And the retailer who sells the boots to you will then raise the price of the to around $125.

On the other end of the spectrum is the domestic, high-end specialty manufacturer that must sell its products direct to the consumers. If it used the same distribution method as the mass marketer, those same boots would have to be priced at around $350 to make the same profit margin for the manufacturer. One of the main advantages of buying from a domestic manufacturer is that the manufacturer can stand behind its product and make repairs down the road. Quality control is also easier when the items are manufactured on the company's premises rather than on the other side of the planet.

Materials

One of the biggest decisions to make when purchasing a piece of riding gear is deciding on the material. Natural hides have traditionally been the choice of motorcycle riders because they are abrasion resistant and durable. This is why virtually all racing suits are made of leather. But all leathers are not the same. Elkskin, deerskin, and kangaroo are more abrasion and tear resistant than cowhide and, unlike cowhide, can be washed without getting hard and dry. Of course, they are also more expensive. Kangaroo has the highest strength-to-weight ratio, but because it is so thin, a small deviation from a given thickness can jeopardize its integrity. It's also difficult to get large pieces of this type of leather, which is why you don't see a lot of one-piece suits made out of kangaroo hide.

When leathers go through the tanning process, the type and amount of dye used is important. Too much dye or the wrong types of it can reduce the strength of the leather and "bleed" on your body. If the dye is completely saturated through the hide, too much of it was used. The amount of bleed also depends on the pH balance of your skin. If you have very acidic skin, it's best to stay with lighter-colored leathers since they won't bleed as much as dark leathers.

Recently, a patented tanning process for leather was introduced, making the hides machine washable and machine dryable. I have been enjoying a jacket like this for several years, and it definitely makes natural hides a much more attractive option.

Natural hides may be the standard motorcycle attire, but synthetic materials are becoming increasingly popular. Synthetic materials generally fall into two categories. The first category is nylon. The second type of synthetic materials are called aramids, although they are better known under their Dupont brand names "Cordura" and "Kevlar."

A good protective garment needs to be tough enough to withstand the abrasive forces of a crash, yet be elastic enough to not let the shearing forces of the road tear it up on impact. This is similar to the way a suspension system keeps the bumps from tearing a motorcycle chassis apart. High-performance nylons have very good strength and are fairly stretchable. Aramids have excellent strength and practically don't stretch at all. This is why suits made with aramids must be blended with a stretchy material like Spandex to allow them the needed flexibility. This blend is generally 30 percent Kevlar and 70 percent Spandex.

Of course, it doesn't do you any good to have strong materials if the thread sewing them together isn't up to the task. When it comes to thread, heavy-duty nylons are generally a better choice than aramids because they can stretch when stressed. When under high loads, non-stretching aramids end up cutting through leather like a cheese knife. So, although the thread is strong, the seam ends up being weak. After seeing hundreds of crashed riding suits and gloves, Z Custom Leather's Adolph Rodrigez says aramid threads don't hold up to abrasion as well as their nylon counterparts.

Construction

How a piece of gear is put together is just as important as what it is made of. Remember, every seam on a garment is a potential weak point. Therefore, the fewer seams, the better. Cheap jackets and pants use many separate pieces of leather because it is cheaper to buy the hides that way. Knowing the ideal suit construction is particularly

The original textile riding suit, the AeroStich Roadcrafter, is still the best suit for street riding you can buy. No other garment matches its combination of comfort, protection, ease-of-use, and utility.

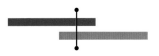

Single Top Stitch
The simplest way to attach fabric should only be used for graphics.

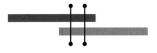

Double Top Stitch
Better for applying patches but too vulnerable to abrasion for major panel joints.

Single Inseam
Typical seam used for gloves where a hidden seam needs to be balanced with minimum bulk.

Double Inseam
Potentially stronger than single inseam with a "second chance" stitch but additional bulk limits options.

Single Inseam with Top Stitch
The minimum seam for joining major protective panels.

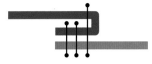

Double Inseam with Top Stitch
One of the best seams for major panels, with two stitches hidden from abrasion damage.

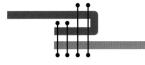

Double Inseam with Double Top Stitch
When properly done, this is the strongest seam for joining protective panels, but so many holes in the leather risk perforation tears.

The best gear is transparent to the rider, effortlessly following his lead and never getting in the way.

important if you are thinking of adding graphics to your attire. It is much wiser to have the graphics as thin appliqués on top of the leather than to cut the pattern of the suit based on the graphic elements. It's always more expensive to add graphics rather than just change colors along the natural lines of the suit's pattern.

The stitching style is just as important as the thread material and construction patterns. There are many types of seams (figure 1), and the more strength a seam needs, the more important it is that it be shielded from outside abrasion.

It should be noted that every hole you put in leather makes it weaker. Many garments use too many stitches within too little space, often using tiny thread that turns

Good gloves should have extra protection in the high-abrasion areas of the knuckles and palm. A seamless palm, like the one on these DeerSports gloves produced by the author, eliminates the discomfort of a seam while being more resistant to coming apart than traditional designs.

All-leather riding boots with replaceable soles like these from Z Custom Leathers are getting harder to find. They can be custom sized and will last for many years if you take care of them.

Fit is never more important than it is when wearing a motorcycle helmet. Some companies like Arai have several internal shapes available in different models so it's best to be fitted by a trained dealer who can help you find the right one.

the seam into the equivalent of perforated paper. Ventilation holes should have at least 0.6 inches of space between each one. If they are any closer than that, the risk of perforation tears is very high.

Armor

The protective padding used in motorcycle apparel varies greatly in terms of its ability to absorb impacts. The best padding uses high-tech foams specifically engineered to turn mechanical energy into heat, covered with stiffer materials to distribute the load over the widest possible surface area of the foam. You want to avoid any padding that doesn't have some flexibility as it will either transfer energy directly to the rider or create high-pressure "hot" spots that will cut or abrade through leather in a crash.

When it comes to back protectors, the most effective designs "bridge" the spine and distribute the load to less fragile parts of the back.

It doesn't matter what the armor is made of if it doesn't stay in place. A lot of the current mesh-type jackets don't have the strength or fit to keep the armor in place during a fall. Of course, if the choice is between a mesh jacket or nothing at all, then some protection is always better than none. While mesh suits may provide adequate protection for sedate riding, if you are going to engage in high performance sport riding you will want apparel that offers more protection

Riding Suits

When it comes to high-performance riding, one-piece suits or zip-together, two-piece suits are a better choice than regular "separates." The reason for this is because in a slide, a non-attached jacket will tend to bunch up, exposing the rider's midsection to abrasion.

Deciding on leather versus textile is a little more difficult. Leather is heavier and warmer on hot days but has better abrasion resistance, with good suits able to be

Custom-fitted suits like this one from Syed Leathers are often no more expensive than high-quality off-the-rack suits, yet can provide a perfect fit. Buying a locally manufactured suit makes getting repairs a whole lot easier.

exception of that on the race track. If you want textile separates but can't quite afford Aerostich quality, Roadgear (www.roadgear.com; 800-854-4327) offers some very good jackets and pants at reasonable prices.

If you're really into track days or racing, leather is your best choice. I highly recommend getting a custom suit from one of the local manufacturers. In the United States, Z Custom, Bates, Vanson, and Syed all make high-quality leathers. There are undoubtedly other good domestic producers but I have not had any personal experience with them. Personally, I have found Vanson to have the best fit and finish. Syed has the most protection, but also has the added weight to go along with it. Bates has the nicest quality leather. And Z has the best service. For the same price as a good set of off-the-rack leathers, do yourself a favor and get them custom made. Not only will they fit you perfectly, but the manufacturers will be able to do repairs on them in the future.

Gloves

Proper fitting gloves are essential for high-performance riding as they are the interface between you and the bike's primary controls. In fact, I feel so strongly about their importance that I began manufacturing my own brand of gloves as I wasn't happy with what was being offered by the major manufacturers.

Because dexterity and feel are so important, you want to have soft, flexible leathers to transmit the most chassis data to the rider. For this reason, the best leathers for gloves are deerskin, elkskin, kangaroo, calfskin, lambskin, and Japanese-dyed cowhide. These soft leathers are prone to stretching so it's important that they fit snugly when you first buy them, or they will become sloppy after you've had them for awhile.

Any true motorcycle glove should have a second protective layer on the high-abrasion areas of the palm and the knuckles. Hard carbon-fiber knuckle "protectors," the current fad in gloves, are a poor choice. This is because upon hard impacts carbon fiber shatters, creating a nasty edge of epoxy-reinforced carbon-fiber "needles" that can penetrate into your hand and other places. If you like the big knuckle look, go for one of the "plastic chrome" versions offered by some manufacturers. As discussed earlier, you should be wary of over-complicated, patched-together designs with tiny threads as they are much more likely to come apart in a crash. Also make sure the gloves have a good retention system so they stay on your hands. Work gloves are designed to come on and off easily so they are not a good choice for riding.

repaired after most crashes. Textile suits, on the other hand, are lighter and more comfortable for casual riding. They are often only good for one serious crash, however, in which case they will sacrifice themselves to save your hide. Remember that even the most expensive suit is less expensive than a skin graft at your local emergency room.

For general street riding, I prefer textile suits as they have features like pockets for storage and are good at accommodating different layer combinations depending on temperature. I'm especially fond of the one-piece Aerostich Roadcrafter (www.aerostich.com; 800-222-1994). Since putting knee pucks put on, I have used this for virtually all my high-performance riding, with the

Boots

Once upon a time not all that long ago it was possible to buy high-quality boots that would last for many years. Nowadays, the market is littered with low-quality boots made of inferior synthetic materials. They are cluttered with lots of cheap plastic do-dads stuck on the outside to try and add back some protection. Unfortunately, some time ago manufacturers learned that if they made fancy looking but non-resoleable boots out of inexpensive materials, they could sell more boots when the originals wore out prematurely.

Fortunately, there are still a few companies, like Z Custom Leathers and Bates, making all-leather sport boots with good ankle padding and replaceable soles. Cruiser and touring riders still have several good options available including Cruiserworks which adds waterproofing to boot.

When trying on boots, make sure they will fit not only your foot, but whatever gear you will be wearing when you ride. For instance, racing leathers have thick shin guards that the boots must fit over. If you have large calves like me, you may have to go custom to get them wide enough. Similarly, if you like to wear your boots under your jeans make sure they won't be too large to fit under the cuffs of your pants. Also check that the boots have enough flexibility in the ankle area for your style of riding.

Helmets

As the single most important piece of safety gear, a helmet is one thing on which you don't want to skimp. The old Bell Helmets advertising slogan still rings true. It read, "If you have a $10 head, wear a $10 helmet."

A proper fitting helmet will be snug but not constricting. It's generally a good idea to go with as small a helmet as you can comfortably wear. This is because the liner will compress over time making it larger, and too large a size can rotate over your eyes or even come off in a crash. Not only is size important, but so is the helmet's internal shape. We all have differently shaped heads, and some helmets will fit your shape much better than others. Some manufacturers even have different liner shapes for different models. The wrong shape will give you headaches at the points of highest pressure.

The more helmets you try on, the better your chances of getting a proper fit. This is why it's best to go to a local dealer. Don't buy mail order unless you know for sure that you fit a particular model. Keep in mind that retailers hate nothing more than being used as a fitting room for a mail order sale. So, try to support your local retailer if he

deserves your business by giving you good service. Don't forget to keep the helmet on for as long as you can in the store because some comfort problems won't show up in the first 30 seconds of wear.

There is a lot of confusion over helmet ratings. The Department of Transportation (DOT) and the Snell Foundation both certify helmets that meet specific criteria relating to impact absorption, shell penetration, retention, and peripheral vision. The Snell standard is a tougher one, and virtually all racing organizations require a helmet that meets the latest guidelines issued by the Snell Foundation. All Snell helmets also pass the DOT test. Some DOT-approved helmets provide adequate protection even though they are not approved by Snell, but you generally can't go wrong with a well-fitting Snell-approved helmet. Under no circumstance should you ever wear a non-DOT-approved helmet.

Unlike body armor or even football helmets, motorcycle helmets are designed to work only once. They absorb energy through the crushing of their foam liners. The purpose of the hard outer shell is to distribute the load over as much of the surface of the foam lining as possible and to protect against penetration. That means that even if the outside shell looks okay, the liner may still be compromised. The bottom line on replacement is if you've been in accident, and your head hit the ground, chances are good you need a new helmet. Most of the helmet manufacturers will give you a free inspection if you want to make sure you really need a new one.

Despite what some manufacturers say, a good helmet can provide up to 10 years of worthwhile protection if, and this is a big if, it was taken care of properly. You can increase the life span of your helmet by never putting it on top of your gas tank and never leaving it in the garage where gas and solvent fumes can degrade the foam liner. Proper care also means never resting the helmet on a mirror, sissy bar, or anything else that puts pressure on a small area of the liner because this will create an indentation. It's also a good idea to periodically clean the comfort liner. Plus, you should also refrain from wearing the same helmet every day so that your helmets will have a chance to breathe.

Arai and Shoei are definitely the best brands of street helmets sold in the United States, and you should seriously consider either one. Suomy and the high-end HJC models also make decent lids that offer very good value. Again, fit is the most important factor here so choose the helmet that fits your head the best. Also remember that with helmets, like most things in life, you get what you pay for.

Chapter 21
Track Days

Every sport rider can benefit from track time. It doesn't matter if you are a race-winning pro, a daily commuter, or a weekend warrior, the more track time, the better. Of course, if you're the professional racer, you get track time forced on you like a third helping of manicotti at Mama Luigi's Italian restaurant. How do the rest of us get served?

Chances are it's a lot easier than you think. The demand for track time has been steadily increasing over the years. All across the world, riding schools and bike clubs have been created or expanded to meet this demand. Ask at your local retailer; there's a good chance that it is sponsoring a day or two at the track this year. Even if it is not directly involved, it should be able to hook you up with a school, riding club, or racing organization that runs on a track somewhere in your area.

If you don't feel like getting close and chummy with someone at the local shop, just enter "Motorcycle Track Day" into a web search engine, and you'll get dozens of hits to browse. With very little effort, you can find a way to get on a nearby race track with your bike. Best of all, this behavior is sanctioned and even legal!

Keep in mind you will need to do some research to locate a group that matches your tastes. There is a group to satisfy everyone's riding appetite. You'll find opportunities that range from under $100 to over $2000.

Control rider Kent Larson points out the apex of a corner to new riders at a NESBA track day.

They range in structure from strict classes that force you into continual lesson drills to open track free-for-alls. Take the time to learn the structure and philosophy of the group with whom you are going to ride and talk it over with friends to make sure you are going to get what you want from the experience.

Why Do It?

The thought of riding on a racetrack generates a lot of questions and concerns: "Am I ready for a track day?" "What bike preparation is needed?" "What should I get for tires?" "Where is the best place to pass?" "What tire pressure should I use?" I'll try to answer these and all the other common concerns. But first, let's address the biggest question of all: "Why would I want to do a track day?"

The street is not the place to learn your limits. You owe it to yourself to separate concerns about pavement conditions, traffic, road debris, and law enforcement so you can focus solely on what you are doing to control your bike.

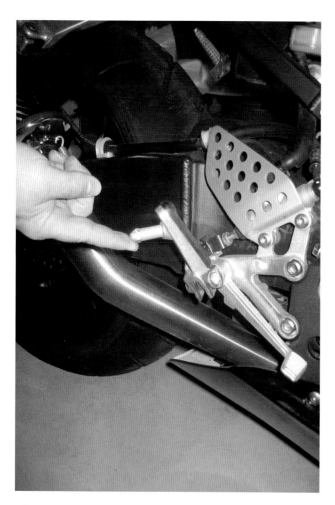

The footpeg feelers are usually the first things to touch down when leaned over in a corner at racetrack speeds.

Depending on the track and the type of track day, you might be required to replace your antifreeze with water. The racetrack surface can become dangerously slippery if antifreeze leaks out of your radiator.

Another advantage of practicing on a track is having the same corner come up every minute or two. This is not just a similar corner like a street ride throws at you every so often, but the exact same corner. You know its radius, bumps, cracks, and all of its other characteristics. Each time through, you can play with your brake point, turn in point, speed, and lean angle without needing to re-evaluate the corner itself each time.

If you already have a comfortable control of the limits, this provides the opportunity to push harder and explore things like how your tires feel when they are sliding. Even if you don't want to get that extreme, the track is still a great place to learn that the limits are often far beyond your comfort levels.

Perhaps early in your riding career you tossed your bike into a left-hand corner and froze, your brain yelling

that you weren't going to make it. Perhaps you went in a bit faster than your comfort level because the rider you were following just tossed it in without touching his brakes and was rapidly pulling away. Now you are fixated on the rapidly approaching guard rail as your bike keeps sweeping along an arc wider than the one followed by the road. Hopefully you made it without expensive bike or body repairs. After a few track days, you will be able to handle that same situation without panicking. The controlled environment of the track will teach you that you are nowhere near your tires' limits and will allow you to just toss it in tighter and stay well clear of the guard rail. Your panic didn't come from being in a marginal situation. It's a result of not knowing how big the margins are.

Track days are not just for the daredevil thrill seekers. They are for everyone. Your current comfort level or type

You may be required to place tape over your headlight to prevent the glass from shattering in case of a mishap. If so, it is a good idea to unplug your headlight to keep the heat of the bulb from turning the tape into a gooey mess.

At a track day you will likely find yourself among riders of widely varying skill levels. As long as everyone follows a few simple precautions, this will not present a significant safety hazard.

of bike does not matter. Get to the track and learn the fine-tuned instinctive control needed to handle emergency situations with calm precise action instead of frozen panic. Even if you don't consider yourself a risk-taker, being in traffic on a motorcycle is going to occasionally throw you a situation that will require you to use all your possible skills to come out safely.

Of course there are those who don't need to be persuaded. The closed-course competition calls to us constantly. Whether it's competition between riders or just the challenge of logging a faster lap time, some people are practically addicted to the track. You, too, may find that the race track pulls you in and doesn't let you go. There are some clubs that count on this. The Northeast Sport Bike Association (NESBA, www.nesba.com) for example, gives you free track time. It allows new members two free, 20-minute rides. Just like your local drug pusher, NESBA gives you your first few hits for free because it knows you'll be back for more.

When I talk to people about track days, I run into some common concerns. They include: "I'm much more likely to crash and wreck my bike if I go to the track."

Really? Why? We are talking about a track day, not a race. There's no reason to go faster than you are comfortable going. The amount of risk you are taking is completely under your control. On the track you don't have on-coming or crossing traffic. Everyone is going

the same direction, and everyone is completely focused on the task of riding. You are not going to share the road with someone reading a book or thinking about dinner or paying more attention to a cell phone conversation than the task at hand. You encounter such situations and worse each time you ride on the street. If you are more likely to crash during a track day than you are when riding on the street, that's because you are taking extra risks and pushing harder on the track. But then, that's the reason some people come to the track, so they can push harder in a safer environment. But just remember, it's your choice.

"I'll just be in everyone's way."

This depends on the club. Some clubs do just toss riders with many different skill levels and bike types out there at the same time. If you are on the slow side in that environment, you just need to worry about yourself. People will get around you without too much trouble, although it may startle you a bit when they pass you. Other clubs group the riders into skill levels and rotate turns so that only the "beginner" group is on the track with you. Typically, a beginner group will also have a strict no-passing or no-passing-except-for-the-front-straight rule in effect. In that case, a really slow rider will hold up the rest of the group, but good clubs will partner that rider with an escort who can direct other riders around the slower bike. This keeps the faster bikes from being frustrated and gives the slower rider help so he can bring up his speeds in a comfortable manner. If this is a concern of yours, be sure to talk to the club director to see if you will fit in comfortably. Most likely you will. There exists a strong desire to assist fellow bikers, and most of your track companions will be more than happy to help keep you comfortable.

Bike Preparation

The requirements for bike preparation will vary from one club to the next. You can take your stock street bike to the NESBA Introductory Class and be out on the track with no changes other than putting a sticker on the front of your bike to show that you've registered and passed tech inspection. Other clubs will require a full race prep including replacing the radiator fluid with distilled water and safety wiring things like your oil plug, oil fill cap, and oil filter. Be sure to get the club rules and have the bike ready before you arrive.

At a minimum, all clubs will require you to have a safe machine, and all should require you to pass through a tech inspection before you are allowed out on the track. If the group you are with doesn't have a tech inspection, you may want to re-consider riding with them. Who knows what will come flying off the hunk-of-junk next to you?

The basics that all clubs should be checking for are:

Useable Tires: At least 75 percent of tread life left. Not cut up or damaged.

Working Brakes, front and back: Good pressure and stopping power. Adequate pad thickness. No fluid leaks. Check for a tight-locking nut on the bottom of the front brake lever pivot bolt.

Nothing Loose: Especially check the clip-on bars, footpegs, and exhaust.

Chain and Sprockets: Make sure the chain and sprocket wear isn't extreme. Check the chain tension. Most street riders run their chains too tight, and the track environment will intensify the problem. Remember your chain tightens as the suspension compresses. At the track, you will use even more of the suspension travel than you do on the street. Set your chain's free play at, or just a bit looser than the manufacturer's recommended setting. Check the manual to see if the specified free play is for when the suspension is compressed under the weight of the rider. A typical mistake is setting the tension without a rider on the bike which makes it much too tight when under load.

Lights: Most track day organizations require you to tape all headlights and taillights. This will help prevent a messy spray of shattered glass if an unfortunate incident occurs. Unplugging your bulbs or pulling their fuses will keep the tape from melting into a gooey mess on the lights and will also help your clean-up process.

Signals and Mirrors: Most clubs ask you to remove your mirrors and turn signals. Even if not asked, removing these items is a good idea.

Some riding clubs require you to replace your anti-freeze. This is always required for race bikes but is rare for track day organizations that cater to the street rider. Asking the street rider to flush the coolant makes the preparation process too involved for many riders and would thin the herd of potential members. It's a good idea, however, to remove all anti-freeze because the spills are nearly impossible to clean up quickly, and they turn pavement sections into non-stick surfaces. If you do change out your anti-freeze, remember to keep your bike in a warm storage facility during the winter. Ice takes up more room than water, and a hard freeze could damage your engine if your radiator contains only water.

Requiring riders to safety wire their bikes might turn away potential track day participants, so it is not always required. Safety wiring is the process of drilling a small hole in the head of a bolt, running a wire through the hole, and wrapping that wire around something else so the bolt isn't allowed to back out or vibrate loose (see appendix). All race bikes are required to have, at a minimum, their oil drain plug, oil fill cap, and oil filter safety wired. Most racing associations also require safety wire on the brake caliper bolts, axle bolts, radiator fill cap, and on many other bolts and fasteners. Even if you don't race your bike and are not required to safety wire for your track day club, it's a good idea to run some wire anyway. Safety wire serves not just to keep a bolt from backing out but it also shows at a glance that you've finished the job. Take, for example, the task of replacing your front tire. By the time you finish, you've tightened the axle bolt, pinch bolts, and caliper bolts to the proper torque. If you safety wire these bolts, you never need to wonder, "Did I tighten the caliper bolts?" A quick look confirms that they are wired, and you will then know that they are tight. The safety wire proves the job was done and assures that it won't get un-done by vibrations.

Frame, bar-end, and swingarm sliders are another consideration as you prepare your soon-to-be-track-bound bike. Aftermarket suppliers now build frame sliders, bar-end sliders, and swing arm sliders specifically for each sportbike model. Having them installed could save a few hundred dollars worth of bodywork during a mishap. Think of it as dressing your bike for the crash. You've

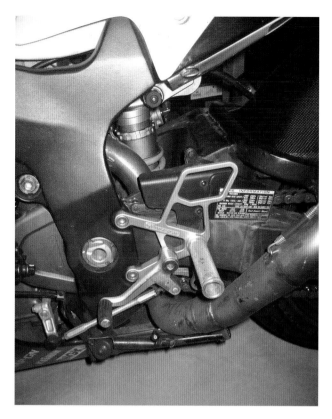

If you have a motorcycle devoted solely to track use, you might want to consider mounting rearset footpegs to increase cornering clearance.

dressed yourself that way, why not be fair and treat your bike to some protection as well? Remember, my contention is that you will be safer on the track than on the street, and the amount of risk is all up to you. However, many of you are taking to the track specifically to push the risk/reward balancing act so make sure you are prepared to handle the possible consequences of accepting that higher risk should you choose to go there.

Check with your club and make sure your bike is ready to pass its tech inspection before you leave for the track. Some clubs will require you to do nothing more than what you should do each time you take your motorcycle out for a street ride. Other clubs will require a full-on race-prep. Just because a club doesn't require all the safety precautions of real racing doesn't mean it's not a good idea.

"What type of tires should I get?"

Track days present an opportunity to run some real race rubber. All the top tire manufacturers offer a DOT race-compound or full-on, race-only slicks to fit any of the racer-replicas. DOT race tires are race-compound

tires that have been cut with a tread so that they are approved by the Department of Transportation for street use. Although approved for street use, I never recommend running a DOT race tire anywhere but at the racetrack. A properly warmed up set of race tires will offer a lap time that's a few seconds better than a set of street rubber or at least give a bigger safety margin at the same lap times. On the race track, you can warm up race tires properly and get them to perform better than street tires. Conversely, running race tires on the street usually results in tires that are never fully warmed up and provide less grip than the appropriate set of street rubber.

If you want to run some race tires, the track is the place. However, if you want to learn more about your street-riding package, this is a chance to test your street tires at their limit. The current crop of high performance street tires will provide more than enough grip for a good rider to lap a lot of the other track day patrons. Just remember, your buddy with the race slicks is going to have a small advantage so don't expect to drive out of

Items like frame sliders (the plastic spool attached to the frame in the fairing vent opening) and case protectors, like the Factory Pro units mounted to this Honda CBR929RR, help limit damage in the event of a crash.

If you are required to safety wire your bike for a track day, you will need to wire the oil drain plug.

the corner at the same speed without spinning just because he is doing it right in front of you.

"What pressure should I run?"

During a street ride, you should run the manufacturer's recommended air pressure to keep a tire from overheating and burning up during a long ride. A track day with its 20- or 30-minute track sessions allows you to lower the pressure a bit and run at optimum temperature to get better grip. Here's a simple way to dial in your tire pressure: Start with between 28 and 34 psi. If the day is cool, somewhere under 60 degrees, start at the low end; if it's hot, 80 degrees or above, start at about 34 psi. Then go out, allow the tires to warm up for a few laps, and start pushing harder. Once you come in, take off your gloves as quickly as possible and feel the tires. If they are cool or mildly warm, they didn't get up to temperature. If this is the case, drop the air pressure by one pound. If the tires are really hot and look like the rubber is boiling and turning a bluish color at the edges, then they got too hot, and you should add a pound or two of air pressure. A tire that is too cold needs less pressure to allow the rubber to bend and stretch. A tire that is too hot needs more pressure so it does less stretching because it's the bending and stretching that generates heat in the tire.

"Are there bikes you can rent for track days?"

Some schools provide fully prepped bikes for their students. For example, Keith Code's California Superbike School has a bike rental option that only costs about $200 more than bringing your own bike. Another option is Freddie Spencer's High Performance Riding School which doesn't even allow riders to bring their own bikes. At Freddie's school, you ride one of the school's Honda CBR600s. If you can afford it, using a school's bike saves you all the trouble of prepping and hauling your own bike. In addition, this gives you the chance to sample a professionally set up suspension which can help you decide if your own ride is dialed or in need of some help.

Rider Preparation

If you want to get the most out of your track time, there's quite a bit of physical and mental preparation that would be beneficial. I'll touch on that in a minute but first let's address the most common concern.

"What do I wear?"

Just like the requirements for bike preparation, the rules for dress vary from club to club, ranging from what would be barely adequate for a street ride all the way to full race-ready gear. Track clubs care about their members and want them in the best protection available, but often the rules are softened to allow a greater number of people to participate. At a minimum, all clubs require a helmet, boots, gloves, and jacket. Some clubs allow you to wear two pairs of jeans, but most require leather pants.

Regardless of your club's requirements, it would benefit you to show up with at least a full-coverage riding outfit. This means either a one-piece or a two-piece that zips together with a full-circumference zipper. A back protector and hard armor in shoulders, knees, and elbows should also be part of your gear. Gloves should be a gauntlet type that extend at least three inches past the wrist. Boots and pant legs should overlap by four or more inches. Your helmet should be less than three years old and have never been dropped or in a crash.

The full-coverage nylon suits are generally accepted and many offer excellent protection in a crash. However, they do tend to be a bit more bulky than a set of leathers and could hinder your ability to move about the bike or get into the ideal body position for aggressive riding. Generally speaking a nylon suit will become more damaged during a crash than a leather suit. They tend to

Another key item to safety wire is your oil filter.

You will also need to safety wire your oil fill cap at track days where safety wiring is required.

melt and develop holes under the friction of a slide, whereas leather just gets a bit scuffed. In other words, nylon suits are only good for one real crash.

Now what about the mental and physical preparations?

It wouldn't hurt to get into good physical shape before your track time. The six or seven half-hour sessions typical of a track day are too much for many of the riders. It is common to have people sit out some of their ride time later in the day because they are just too exhausted.

Fatigue can be partly attributed to mental conditioning rather than physical stamina. For many riders, a track day is a chance to push things to the limit, and many spend a great deal of the time scared silly with a death grip on the bars. Riders who have such an experience are going to be just as slow at the end of the day as they were when they started. It is much better to keep your pace at a comfortable level, increasing things gradually. Staying in your comfort zone and pushing gently on its outer edge will expand your comfort zone

faster than continually bashing against the limit and getting bounced back.

Arm and shoulder fatigue is an indication that you aren't as relaxed as you should be. Even if you aren't having panic moments, you should deliberately relax your upper body every lap or two.

Types of Track Days

Many people come to the track to simply have fun, but most are also there to become better riders. If improving your skills is a goal, make sure you have a plan to reach that goal. That plan will depend quite a bit on what type of track day you are attending.

As mentioned earlier, track days vary widely in cost and philosophy. After finding which clubs or schools fit your schedule, price, and acceptable travel distance, take the time to research each organization's philosophy to make sure it will provide what you desire.

Most track days fit into one of four main classifications:

Open Track Day: "Thanks for your money. Now we'll leave you alone."

Controlled Track Day: "We're not a school, but we're here to help."

Racing or Riding School: "You are here to learn so do what we say."

Race Club: "Sink or swim. Just don't be stupid."

All types of track days will have some rules. Track rules are designed and enforced by the club or school putting on the event rather than by the track itself. If there are any track-specific rules, they will be communicated along with the club/school specific rules. Even the loosest organization needs to lay down a minimum set of rules for safety. If you sign up for a track day and the organization doesn't at least stress the following set of minimum rules, it would be in your best interest to bring them up or stay off the track:

1. There is one and only one location to enter the track.
2. There is one and only one location to exit the track.
3. All track traffic goes in one direction. You must never, ever travel on the track in the reverse direction.
4. You must never stop on the track surface.
5. If you have a problem and must slow down, you should raise your left arm or kick out a foot to let approaching riders know you are slowing down.

Open Track Days

Open track days are the least structured and usually least expensive form of track time. Cost is typically $100 to $200 for a day. The day is put on by a group of riders or a dealership or even an entrepreneurial individual that has worked out a track rental arrangement. Track rules at open track days are usually pretty lax or non-existent. A rogue rider can spoil the day if no clear authority steps up to stop him. Your comfort at this type of day can vary greatly depending on the makeup of the group. An experienced group of self-policing riders will keep things smooth. A loose group of wild idiots could make things hairy. Of course, if you are one of the wild idiots, this could give you the freedom to ride the way you want without all the pesky barriers like common sense, traffic laws, politeness, or civility.

Any open track day organized by an experienced individual or group will have kicked out or curtailed the wilder members, but such track days are still not for everyone. If you are a slower rider, you need to be comfortable with getting passed at any time before you venture out on the track. If you are a faster rider, you need to be competent passing slower riders. As in racing, it's always the responsibility of the rider passing and not the rider being passed to make sure the pass is safe.

"Where's the best place to pass?"

When participating in open track days, one should follow a few basic principles regarding passing. First, there is no one best place to pass. Each track will offer different passing zones. Passing decisions are dependent on the situation. Keep in mind that during a track day, there isn't any prize for finishing in front of that rider you are trying to pass. If you can't decide on a safe passing zone but are frustrated by being held up mid-corner, simply exit the track and come back on just in front of him a lap later. Or, let the slower rider pull a gap by holding back on a few straights. Of course, that's not nearly as satisfying as blowing past him and giving a wave as you disappear down the track, so if you are an experienced rider, it is quite likely that you'll find yourself passing a slower rider.

The safest pass is one where you are passing while the other bike is moving away from you, not toward you. For instance, you can set up a rider who corners slower than you by letting him pull a small gap before the turn starts, then closing in on him through the turn. You will need to time it so you are passing on the inside as the slower rider drifts wide at the exit. That way, the slower rider is away from you, toward the outside of the track, and you've got more speed and a line that's a bit to the inside. This, however, gets you nothing if the other rider is able to crack open a 140-horsepower engine next to your 50-horsepower bike once you are both fully upright.

You might also be able to come up the inside on the brakes as the other rider is drifting out to set up his turn-in. This again will provide an opportunity where the slower rider is moving away from you as you pass. Just keep in mind that you want to avoid putting your bike on an intersecting line with another rider. If passing or being passed is an overwhelming concern or fear that keeps you from participating in open track days, you may want to consider a controlled track day.

Controlled Track Days

Controlled track days provide a bit more structure without too much added cost. Groups that organize controlled track days have experienced riders on the track to keep things in control and to help riders who want riding instruction. An example of this is NESBA.

NESBA breaks its members into three classes: beginner, intermediate, and expert. The beginners are lead around the track in small groups behind a "control rider." The control rider's job is to demonstrate the proper line through the corners and to make sure the riders following her are comfortable. As the day goes on,

Provided you exercise some common sense, you will find that riding on a racetrack can be safer than riding on the street.

the pace is gradually increased. Beginners are not allowed to pass control riders and can pass other members only on designated areas of the track.

The intermediate group of riders is also on the track with a handful of control riders. In the intermediate group, you are allowed to pass other members anywhere on the track except in a corner, but you are still not allowed to pass a control rider. In this group, the control riders are working on riding techniques with members who ask for help and keeping a watch out for undesired behavior.

The expert group is free of the control riders and has no rules about passing other than to keep the passes "safe." The control riders for the beginning and intermediate groups will run in this group when they want track time without the responsibility of the control rider job.

Riding with a group like NESBA is comfortable for every rider of every ability because the control riders are there to help make sure everyone is content. Slower riders are under supervision, and faster riders are waved past when safe. This, however, can become frustrating for some riders who are on the border between groups. The fastest beginners will

sometimes find themselves blocked by the slower members and have to wait for the designated passing zone. Usually, this is alleviated by graduating to the next faster class after passing an evaluation by a control rider captain.

The beginner and intermediate groups in organizations like NESBA contain far too much structure for some riders, but even the most experienced riders will enjoy riding with the fastest of the groups. If a rider is frustrated by the structure but isn't able to demonstrate the ability to qualify for the fastest group, these clubs are not for him.

Racing or Riding Schools

Racing or riding schools vary widely. Some schools are structured to the point that riders do nothing but skill drills all day. Other schools have classroom sessions between track sessions. A track school is something that should be thoroughly researched before a rider commits the time and money. Don't sign up for a school without reading a review or discussing it with someone you trust and who has taken the class. My personal recommendations are in the appendix.

Some people do not have the desire or the discipline to run skill drills all day regardless of how much it will improve their riding skills. Some people will be disappointed if they don't get any one-on-one instruction time. These schools cost too much and have too much variation in style to jump into them without first doing some research

Racing Clubs

There are racing clubs all across the United States. Actually, there are racing clubs all across the world. I know a guy who races his CBR900RR in Russia, and my buddy Ivan runs an R6 race bike in the Netherlands. It seems that anywhere you get enough testosterone and internal combustion engines together, a race is going to break out. You can find outlets for racing your riding lawn mower or your unicycle, so it should be no surprise that there are places to race your motorcycle.

A racing club is a giant step above the local street racing "Biker Boyz" scene when it comes to organization and safety. There are regional and national clubs that range from entry level up to the professional ranks. The web site for Road Racing World and Motorcycle Technology (www.roadracingworld.com) has an "Organizations" page which lists clubs in the United States. The entry level clubs are open to anyone willing to wire up their bike, while the pro organizations require some proof of past performance before they will give you a license.

It's absurdly easy to join and qualify for a race license in most club racing organizations. Check the back of *Road Racing World and, Motorcycle Technology*, or *Cycle News* to find a club that races on a track near you and sign up for its new-rider school. You'll get a day with some track time and some classroom time to prepare for racing. The school will teach you the meaning of the different flags and perhaps give you some pointers about how to ride. At the end of the day, you'll be "gridded" up for a new-rider's race. Typically, all that is required for a license is to finish the race without doing something stupid like taking out another rider or crashing.

Any idiot with a street bike and a few hundred bucks can end up with a racing license. However, you will need to get the club's rule book and make sure your bike passes its requirements. Requirements will include replacing the anti-freeze with water; removing all the lights, signals, and mirrors; and safety wiring the club's required bolts and fasteners. Many people start with a street bike and the idea that they will prep it for race weekends but return it to the street afterwards. This usually lasts about one or two weekends. After that, the motorcycle often becomes a dedicated race bike.

The reward for getting a race license is a lot of cheap track time. For example, the Central Roadracing Association, or CRA (www.cra-mn.org), usually offers a full day of practice on Fridays before a race weekend for just $50.

Another reward is the competition itself. Some people thrive in the racing environment. Last year, a friend went from being a fast street rider to a track junky and finally a licensed racer with the CRA. At each transition, he was awestruck by the realization of what he was missing before taking the step into competition. As a street rider, he couldn't believe a track could offer any more fun than he was already having. He got to the track and couldn't believe how much more you could push the limits in a controlled environment. Looking back, he believed that street riding stuff was nothing in comparison to racing. Then he got his racing license and learned the difference between pushing hard because he wanted to see if he could and because he wanted to beat that rider in front of him. Racing isn't for everyone, but some will find there's nothing nearly as satisfying as racing.

Just Do It!

Search the web, ask your retailer, talk to friends, join a local riding club, or just inquire at a nearby track to get a list of clubs and schools that will provide track time on nearby tracks. Then do some research on the group you want to join. Most importantly, get thee to a track! You will not regret it. Ok, if you crash, you might regret it. So don't do that.

There is no other place to really find out what you and your bike can do than a track. It doesn't matter if you are just starting out or if you think you're the fastest thing to hit the streets. Go to the track and see what you are missing. It will pay you back with skills and knowledge you can use on every ride, whether on the track or the street.

Appendix

Motorcycle Schools Listing

The following listing includes both street and track oriented schools. For those interested in track days, the best resource is www.trackday.com, which lists track days by track and by racing school. Riders can also sign up for track days around the country right from the site. It is an excellent resource. Schools with an asterisk(*) by that name are my personal recommendations.

American Supercamp

Danny Walker's dirt-based school uses Honda XR100s in a safe, comfortable atmosphere with plenty of seat time and video feedback of your riding. While the cornering techniques are designed for the dirt and shouldn't be used on the road, there is no better way for street riders to learn how to control a sliding motorcycle. It's also a lot of fun.

553 Lakewood Ct.
Windsor, CO 80550
(970) 674-9434
www.americansupercamp.com

AFM—American Federation of Motorcyclists

This California-based organization caters to the weekend racer. The AFM is the oldest organization in the country dedicated to motorcycle road racing. It operates a race school and runs practices and races. All races are part of a championship points series that culminates each season in an awards banquet where the season's class champions are presented with year-end awards.

6167 Jarvis Ave. #333
Newark, CA 94560
www.afmracing.org

CLASS

At CLASS, Reg Pridmore focuses on teaching you how to become a smoother, safer, and more confident rider with instruction on more effective braking, shifting, cornering, and how to avoid some pitfalls that often occur as a result of bad habits.

320 E. Santa Maria Street, Suite M
Santa Paula, CA 93060-3800
www.classrides.com

Cornerspeed

Cornerspeed is the official rider school for VIR (Virginia International Raceway). Fully accredited by WERA and CCS, students that complete the course are eligible for their provisional racing license.

(704) 332-3147
www.cornerspeed.net

DP Safety School

This California-based, street-oriented track school counts many former race champions among its instructors.

PO Box 1551
Morro Bay CA 93443-1551
(805) 772-8301
www.dpsafetyschool.com

Ed Bargy Racing School

This racing school based in the Southeast is for riders interested in obtaining a race license.

337 Johnson Brady Rd
Canton, GA 30115
(770) 345-6474
www.edbargyracingschool.com

Fastrack Riders

This California-based, weekend racer organization organizes track days around four levels of riders, from beginner to club racer.

P.O. Box 129
San Juan Capistrano, CA 92693-0129
(877) 560-2233
www.fastrackriders.com

Fasttrax

Fasttrax has two schools, one oriented for street skills and the other for those interested in club racing. Based around the Nelson Ledges racetrack in Ohio.

(330) 494-8410
www.fastone.com

Frank Kinsey

Similar to Ed Bargy Racing School, the Kinsey school is designed for those who wish to obtain a race license.

(321) 267-4787
www.kinseyracingschool.com

Freddie Spencer's High Performance Riding School

Taught by three-time world champion Freddie Spencer, the Spencer school has both street- and racing-oriented classes. The top racing classes use on-board telemetry so students can see exactly what they are doing and even compare individual turns from lap to lap. All classes are held at the Las Vegas Motor Speedway.

7055 Speedway Blvd. Suite E
Las Vegas, NV 89115
(702) 643-1099
www.fastfreddie.com

California Superbike School

The original high-performance riding school designed by world champion trainer Keith Code is still the most innovative of them all. The painstakingly well-researched curriculum includes braking and cornering trainers. The school uses four separate levels of training to appeal to both racers and street enthusiasts.

940 San Fernando Road
Los Angeles, CA 90065
(323) 224-2734
www.superbikeschool.com

Kevin Schwantz Suzuki School

Former 500GP champion Kevin Schwantz teaches skills for both street and track riding using Suzuki motorcycles. The school is based at Road Atlanta.

(800) 849-RACE
www.Schwantzschool.com

Learning Curves Racing

This is a race-oriented school based out of Wisconsin.
2219 S. 57th Street
West Allis, WI 53219
(414) 327-0140
www.learningcurves.com

Mid Atlantic Road Racing Club

This racing school is held at Summit Point, West Virginia.
(301) 791-6167
marrc.nova.org

Mike Sullivan Road Racing School

This race-oriented school is based out of Washington
3508 Fords Pr. Ave.
Centralia, WA 98531
(360) 736-2791
www.sullivanraceschool.com

Penguin

One of the oldest race oriented schools around, the Penguin school has been in existence for 32 years. The school is primarily based in New Hampshire, though several dates in Florida are also held.

347 Pratt St
Mansfield, MA 02048
(508) 339-4673
www.penguinracing.com

STAR

Run by AMA champion Jason Pridmore, the California-Based STAR School is divided into two groups. The first group is for street riders and newcomers to the track, and the other for more advanced students and those with track experience who wish to explore their limits with fewer restrictions.

4587 Telephone Rd. #206
Ventura, CA 93003-5653
www.starmotorcycle.com

Team Hammer Advanced Riding School

Also know as the Suzuki Advanced Riding School, Team Hammer is oriented toward riders who aspire to race competitively.

P.O. Box 183
Wildomar CA 92595
(909) 245-6414
www.teamhammer.com

Team Pro Motion

A race-oriented school, organized around three skill-level schools instead of separate classes of the same track school, Team Pro Motion frequents various tracks along the northeast and east-central seaboard.

550 H West Street Road
Warminster, PA 18974
(215) 671-8660
www.teampromotion.com

U.S. Magazines covering High-Performance Riding

Cycle News—www.cyclenews.com.
Weekly racing coverage along with reviews and interviews.

Cycle World—www.cycleworld.com.
Street and dirt coverage with special attention paid to sportbikes and technical commentaries by Kevin Cameron.

Friction Zone—www.friction-zone.com.
California-based publication with monthly riding skills stories.

Motorcyclist—www.motorcyclistonline.com.
General interest street bike magazine with monthly riding tips.

Motorcycle Consumer News—www.mcnews.com.
Black and white consumerist publication doesn't accept advertising and features monthly riding skills stories.

Roadracing World & Motorcycle Technology—venus.13x.com/roadracingworld/index.html. The most comprehensive road racing monthly with excellent tech stories.

Sport Rider—www.sportrider.com.
Sportbike coverage with monthly riding tips.

Rider—www.riderreport.com.
Touring and cruising focus with monthly riding skills stories.

E-Zines

2WF.com—www.2wf.com
Cycle News—www.cyclenews.com
Motorcycle News—www.motorcyclenews.com
Motorcycle Daily—www.motorcycledaily.com
Motoworld.com—motoworld.com
Motorworld—www.motorworld.com
AMASuperbike.com—www.amasuperbike.com
Motorcycle Online—www.motorcycle.com
Powersportnetwork.com—
    www.powersportsnetwork.com
Sportbikes.Com—www.sportbikes.com

Other Useful Websites

http://www.eurospares.com
Eurospares is a website devoted to homemade specials. Many discussion groups full of extremely talented people. This should be one of your first stops if you are interested in chassis design. Many photos of specials, links to other useful sites, list of suggested reading, etc.

www.europark.com
Photos and specs for GP bikes.

www.engineersedge.com
Lots of interesting engineering information.

www.howstuffworks.com
Self-explanatory.

Electronic Mailing Lists

Carl Paukstis maintains the most comprehensive listing of electronic mailing lists for motorcyclists in the world called the Mailing List Roundup. The list can be viewed online at http://www.micapeak.com. Two of the most appropriate track-oriented references are offered below. The Mailing List Roundup outlines mailing lists based on marque, model, and style of riding. These lists are vital for anyone wishing to gain information on their bikes, their favorite marque, or style of riding. Most lists have a FAQ (frequently asked questions listing) to answer basic questions for new members. Micapeak also features a registry of motorcycles that is extremely useful for learning of problem areas of any one given motorcycle.

Suspension and Bike Handling Part Vendors

Smart riders spend money on suspension upgrades before spending on cosmetic goodies. Dollar for dollar, suspension is a much better investment in performance than engine and exhaust mods.

Fox Racing Shocks—www.foxracingshox.com
GPR Steering Stabilizers—www.gprstabilizer.com
Ohlins—www.ohlins.com
Penske—www.penskeshocks.com
Progressive Suspension—www.progressivesuspension.com
Race Tech—www.race-tech.com
Lindemann Suspension—www.le-suspension.com
Traxxion Dynamics—www.traxxion.com
Engineered Racing Products—www.engineeredracingproducts.com
WP suspension—www.whitebros.com
G.M.D. Computrack—www.gmdcomputrack.com

Pre-ride checklist

The MSF (Motorcycle Safety Foundation) stresses the importance of checking one's equipment prior to any ride. Unfortunately, most riders are in a hurry to don their helmet, start their bike, and begin their journey. Motorcycles require more attention to detail than cars do. It pays to take a few minutes to inspect the functionality of your motorcycle prior to any ride. Use this checklist to prepare you and your bike for the day's riding fun.

Motorcycle Inspection

Tire pressure and condition

Inspect the front tire carefully for cupping. If present, cupping will be felt when braking, when it will create the impression that the front end is shimmying.

Use recommended tire pressures for the bike and the tire manufacturer. When the two numbers differ, always go with the tire manufacturer's recommended pressure.

Mirrors—positioned properly and clean

Oil level and coolant level

Brake and clutch actuation

Lights and turn signals function

Chain tensioned and lubed

Indicator lights on instrument panel function

Disk lock removed (place a piece of tape over the ignition switch to remind you to remove the disc lock)

Rider

Faceshield—free of dirt and scratches

Helmet fits properly

Jacket fits properly—loose jackets will cause buffeting that can be very distracting

Gloves don't bind when hand is curved into riding position.

No loose shoestrings—loose strings can get caught up in the shift and brake levers

Rider is alert and free of stimulants or depressants.

Recommended Reading

Smart riders treat their sport as both a hobby and an intellectual pursuit. My recommended reading list will get you up to speed on most facets of performance riding and tuning.

Proficient Motorcycling by David Hough. Lots of useful riding info and strategies for staying safe on the street.

Soft Science of Road Racing Motorcycles by Keith Code. A must for competitive roadracers.

Sportbike Performance Handbook by Kevin Cameron. A fantastic overview of building a high-performance motorcycle.

The Motorcycle Safety Foundation's Guide to Motorcycling Excellence: Skills, Knowledge, and Strategies for Riding Right, 2nd ed. by Nate Rauba. A good reference for beginning riders who want a better understanding of how their bikes work and basic riding strategies.

Twist of the Wrist by Keith Code. The original high-performance riding manual and still one of the best.

Twist of the Wrist II by Keith Code. A must-have skills book for all high-performance riders.

Machinery's Handbook by Erik Oberg, et al. This is the bible of mechanical design. It includes everything you ever wanted to know about how to make things. This book is on every good mechanical engineer and machinist desk.

The Shock Absorber Handbook by John C Dixon. Very good work on shocks, but written by an engineer for engineers. Yes it does have advanced math.

Motorcycle Chassis Design: The Theory and Practice by Tony Foale and Vic Willoughby. This is the classic work on the subject.

www.tonyfoale.com

Motorcycle Handling and Chassis Design by Tony Foale. Tony's latest work with up-to-date references and unique insights.

The Racing Motorcycle—A technical guide for constructors, Volume 1 by John Bradley.

This is an excellent work on basic motorcycle design. Some math is involved.

www.eurospares.com

Essential Track Day Packing List

There are a number of things you can take to the track to enhance your experience. Get a printout of the layout of the track and study each turn. While it is hard to get a feel for the track from a picture, you can get a rough idea from the length of the straightaways, the number of turns, and the severity of each turn.

Find out what amenities are at the track, such as whether or not the access along pit row where you will have to park is paved. Are there electrical outlets and facilities?

Pack any specialized tools needed to perform basic services on your bike, such as axle nut wrenches and preload spanners. If you frequent a track more than several times each year, you may wish to purchase a separate set of tools just for the track and leave them packed in a separate "track day" toolbox. In addition to basic tools, maintenance aids should also be packed, including front and rear bike stands, spare oil, chain lube, and a supply of rags. Finally, many tracks do not have fuel pumps, so pack a spare can of gas to make it through the afternoon sessions.

In addition to tools, I recommend a host of both essential and comfort-oriented items. First and foremost is a collapsible awning. These awnings are generally 10-feet-by-10-feet or 10-feet-by-20-feet in size and can be assembled in minutes. They are essential for keeping the sun off a leather-clad rider in the pits, especially during the summer months. You may consider two awnings, one for shade for the motorcycles and one for the riders and crew. In addition to an awning, several folding chairs and a high-velocity fan will allow your pit crew to relax while you dry your socks off. You may wish to bring your own portable air tank in case your tires are underinflated. The one I bring is usually borrowed by several riders on the track. Finally, consider taking a push broom to keep the work area clean around those sticky tires.

One last set of items to pack falls into the "safety related" category. This includes a first aid kit, a fire extinguisher, and beverages (preferably water instead of sodas) to keep the riders and pit crew hydrated.

You may not be required to safety wire your motorcycle, but doing so will prevent parts falling off your bike at the most inopportune moments.

Experienced track day visitors usually bring many other items to make the experience more like a camping trip, everything from bar-b-que grills to beach blankets and binoculars. If you attend enough track days, you'll find that they can require more planning and preparation than most camping trips. This isn't necessarily a bad thing, because track days can be more fun than camping.

Safety Wire How-To

Safety wire is the next best thing to duct tape and zip ties. Unfortunately, conventional wisdom holds that safety wiring is only appropriate for track bikes. Hogwash, I say. Safety wiring is appropriate for any machine that you want to hold together—and high-performance motorcycles certainly qualify. In fact, I safety wire all my bikes, regardless of whether they are track tools or not. Not only is safety wire preventative medicine, it is also essential for securing bolts that are frequently removed. Bolts that are candidates for safety wiring include the following:

Brake caliper retention bolts
Brake pad retention pins
Fork pinch bolts
Triple tree bolts
Oil fill cap
Coolant fill cap
Oil drain plug
Banjo bolts

Safety wiring is NOT a replacement for a fastener. Also, improper technique can make the safety wire useless. Safety wire comes in three thicknesses: .02-inch, .032-inch, and .041-inch, and is available from most hardware stores. However, for motorcycling, the wire should be nickel-coated to resist corrosion. Most hardware store safety wire does not have a nickel coating on the outside of the steel. The thicker the wire, the less prone it is to break while twisting. Some guidelines specify the optimal number of twists per inch, but giving such a number is inappropriate due to the relative thickness of the safety wire. The wire will let you know when it is getting stressed from being turned too many times by snapping.

The key to installing safety wire is to be patient, use the proper technique, and use a set of safety wire pliers. Before you begin, you will need to drill a small 1/16-inch hole through the bolt that you wish to wire. With this size of hole, you can use all three gauges of wire. Having a bolt jig to hold the bolt while you drill helps accomplish the task., You can use a spring-loaded punch to mark a dot for the drill bit to use as a

The tools needed to do the job. A drill, a 1/16" drill bit, safety wire pliers, safety wire and some small blunt-end wire cutters for reaching out-of-the-way spots.

Always tension the safety wire in the direction of the bolt's tension.

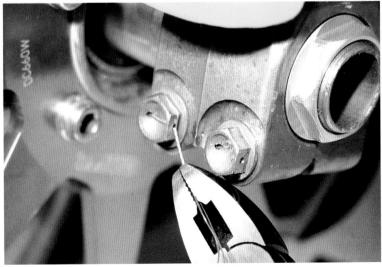

You can wire to a fixed point on the motorcycle . . . . or to another bolt.

starting point. The drill bit will only last for a few holes unless you find a way to keep the bit cool while drilling. While some riders use water, I prefer to keep a fresh supply of oil sprayed on the bit to help keep it cool.

Once you have drilled a hole completely through the bolt, install the bolt and torque it to specification. Find a securing point on the motorcycle to which you can safety wire the bolt. Engine cooling fins, other bolts, or any hard-mount area is suitable as a mounting point for the safety wire. The key thing to remember is that the bolt should be wired so that the safety wire

keeps the bolt tensioned. That way the bolt will not be able to work itself loose and unwind.

Care must be taken when installing the safety wire. Small nicks in the wire will compromise its longevity. Nicks often occur when pulling the wire through the hole or when the wire gets pinched while twisting. It takes some practice to become adept at wiring, but the wire is cheap, and with practice you can make your safety wiring as attractive as any other part of the motorcycle.

Garage Stuff

The list below includes what I recommend for the optimal garage setup. This list of recommended tools only includes the non-standard tools that make maintenance much easier. After you have acquired all the tools you need, you should pay attention to how your garage is laid out. By being efficient in how you store your stuff, you will avoid what I call "clutter creep." I define clutter creep as the tendency for stuff to attract more stuff. A classic example is your garage floor. Once you begin laying things around, the tendency is to lay more things around those already out of place. Before you know it, all available floor space is occupied by a tool or part. You can avoid this tendency by storing things in their proper place and keeping them off the floor. Square footage of garage space is a scarce commodity for most shade tree mechanics.

Basic maintenance and modification tools
- Vise and "C" clamps
- Grinder
- Plastic bottle (with rubber hosing for carburetor synchs with the gas tank off)
- Carb Synch sticks or gauges
- Vacuum pump
- Battery charger
- Battery tester
- Plastic welder
- Compression tester
- Leak down tester

- Drill press
- Acetylene torch
- Arc welder
- Balancing stand
- Dremel tool kit
- Tap and die set
- Magnifying jewelers light
- Magnetic pickup tool
- Bore and hone kit
- Piston ring expanders and compressors
- Gear pullers
- Air compressor
- Air ratchet and wrench
- Tire bead breaker
- Front and rear bike stands
- Engine stand
- Brake bleeder
- Bead blasting cabinet
- Parts washer
- Dehumidifier
- Digital calipers
- Digital micrometer
- Bike lift
- Bike hoist
- Seal driver kit
- Ear plugs
- Safety glasses

Index

**Ducati Desmoquattro
Performance Handbook**
ISBN 0-7603-1236-2

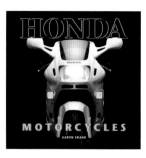

Honda Motorcycles
ISBN 0-7603-1077-7

Streetbike Extreme
ISBN 0-7603-1299-0

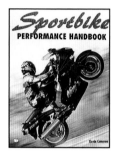

**Sportbike
Performance Handbook**
ISBN 0-7603-0299-4

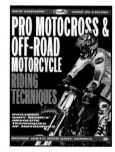

**Pro Motorcross and Off-Road
Riding Techniques**
ISBN 0-7603-0831-4

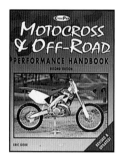

**Motocross and Off-Road
Performance Handbook**
ISBN 0-7603-0660-5

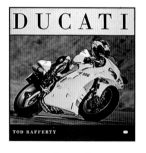

Ducati
ISBN 0-7603-0663-X

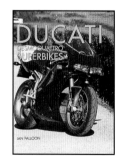

**Ducati Desmoquattro
Superbikes**
ISBN 0-7603-1309-1

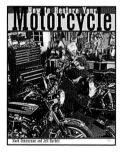

**How to Restore
Your Motorcycle**
ISBN 0-7603-0681-8